THE TEACHER'S

2

IDEA
BOOK

Planning Around
CHILDREN'S
INTERESTS

Other Title in Series

The Teacher's Idea Book: Daily Planning Around the Key Experiences

Related High/Scope Press Preschool Publications

Educating Young Children: Active Learning Practices for Preschool and Child Care Programs

Supporting Young Learners 1: Ideas for Preschool and Day Care Providers

Supporting Young Learners 2: Ideas for Child Care Providers and Teachers

High/Scope Extensions, Newsletter of the High/Scope Curriculum

High/Scope Buyer's Guide to Children's Software, 11th Ed.

Adult-Child Interactions: Forming Partnerships With Children (video)

Drawing and Painting: Ways to Support Young Artists (video)

Available from
HIGH/SCOPE PRESS
600 North River Street, Ypsilanti, Michigan 48198-2898
313/485-2000, Fax 313/485-0704

Planning Around
CHILDREN'S INTERESTS

THE TEACHER'S

2

IDEA
BOOK

Michelle Graves

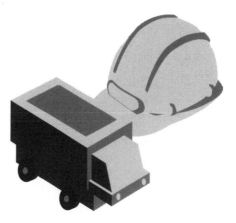

HIGH/SCOPE PRESS
Ypsilanti, Michigan

PUBLISHED BY
High/Scope® Press
A division of the
HIGH/SCOPE EDUCATIONAL RESEARCH FOUNDATION
600 NORTH RIVER STREET
YPSILANTI, MICHIGAN 48198-2898
313/485-2000, FAX 313/485-0704

Editors: Nancy Altman Brickman, Lynn Taylor
Cover Design: Margaret FitzGerald
Text Design: Margaret FitzGerald
Photography: Gregory Fox

Library of Congress Cataloging-in-Publication Data

Graves, Michelle, 1952
        The teacher's idea book.

        Bibliography: p.
        1. Education, Preschool--Curricula--Handbooks,
manuals, etc. 2. Education, Preschool--Handbooks,
manuals, etc. 3. Day care centers--Handbooks, manuals,
etc. I. Title.
LB1140.4.G73 1989   372.19'0202   88-35794
ISBN 1-57379-019-2

Printed in the United States of America
10 9 8 7

Contents

3 Pretend Play: Favorite Play Roles 33

4 Nature: Observing Plants, Animals, and Weather 51

5 Social Play: Exploring Feelings and Relationships 69

6 Celebrations: Experiencing Holidays and Special Events 89

7 "Messy" Materials: Pouring, Filling, Mixing, and Molding 109

8 Food-Related Play: Cooking, Eating, and Pretending 127

9 Character Play: Pooh, Piglet, and Power Rangers 145

Preface

This book grows out of my experiences working with children in the High/Scope Demonstration Preschool in Ypsilanti, Michigan. As a teacher who returned to direct work with children after spending 12 years as a teacher-trainer and child care administrator, I think I have a unique perspective to share with other teachers who are seeking ways to make their programs more responsive to young children's interests. When I resumed teaching in the Demonstration Preschool three years ago, I felt both excitement and anxiety about the responsibility of providing a positive learning environment for children on a day-by-day basis. Heightening these feelings was my awareness that new elements had been added to the High/Scope approach since I had last used it as a teacher. Since I had not yet had hands-on experience with these newer elements, I approached my return to teaching with the nervousness of a new teacher on her first day of school.

One of these newer aspects of the High/Scope approach is an increased emphasis on planning and teaching around children's interests. My experiences in teaching from this new perspective over the past several years have convinced me that children's interests are a rich source of teaching ideas. When we incorporate our observations about children's interests throughout the daily routine, children's enthusiasm and engagement grow and their opportunities for learning multiply. In this book I've shared some of the actual classroom experiences I've participated in and observed as I've grown more attuned to the interests children express in their conversation and play. I've used these experiences to illustrate the exciting things that happen when adults are committed to a child-oriented planning process. My hope is that this book will be helpful to those who strive to understand, interpret, and implement the High/Scope approach in their educational settings.

Many people have encouraged and supported me as I worked on this book. Mark Tompkins stimulated me to begin writing by encouraging me to clarify what "planning around children's interests" really meant. Mary Hohmann, Lynn Taylor, and Philip Hawkins supported me throughout the earliest stages of writing with their suggestions for organizing the material and developing a format for the book. Once the book was in draft form, David Weikart, Mary Hohmann, and Linda Weikel offered many invaluable suggestions that have enriched and improved the content. Special thanks go to my editor, Nancy Brickman, whose understanding of the content and talent for rephrasing while maintaining the ideas in the original text are reflected throughout the pages that follow. I'd also like to acknowledge Barbara Carmody, Carol Beardmore, Julie Austin, and Sam Hannibal, who at various times served as my co-teachers, for the teaching ideas they contributed during our daily planning meetings.

Finally, I'd like to thank my husband, Keith, and our preschool-aged children, Christopher and Joshua. Their spirit and sense of adventure showed me, in a personal way, the benefits of including children's interests and ideas in the teaching process.

—M.G.

Introduction  1

Learning how to plan and teach based on children's interests is the focus of this book. This child-oriented planning process takes place in preschool learning environments designed according to the principles of the High/Scope active learning approach. If you are not familiar with the basic principles of this approach, we suggest that you first read the summary of the High/Scope framework presented on pages 4–11 before proceeding.

The High/Scope approach to planning for the day-to-day content of an early childhood program differs in important ways from other common approaches to curriculum planning. In many preschools, teachers organize their programs by developing weekly or monthly lesson plans focused on child-oriented topics such as "dinosaurs" or "community helpers." In other preschools teachers use a child development framework as the basis for planning, and develop teaching units focused on specific ability areas, such as letter recognition or number concepts.

By contrast, in the High/Scope approach **planning starts with specific observations of children** rather than with a predetermined set of topics. Each day teachers observe children to see what activities and materials they choose, how they work with the materials, and how they interact with peers and adults. As they observe children, teachers jot down brief anecdotal notes on their observations. Later they meet to develop plans for the next day's program based on these observations and the framework of the High/Scope approach.

High/Scope teachers consider many factors as they carry out this planning process. One of these is thinking about the environment: how to provide spaces and

In the High/Scope approach, planning starts as teachers observe children's specific interests. One day, Donald makes up a game using cardboard tubes and tennis balls. Observing this, Donald's teacher creates a game for the next day's planning time that uses a similar set of materials. In this game, individual children describe their plans, then drop a small ball down the tube into a bowl, choosing the bowl that represents the interest area where they want to work. (The sheets of paper in the bowls display area symbols.)

materials where children can fill and empty, be messy, build, pretend, and have quiet times, because these are essential learning activities that young children enjoy. As they plan, teachers also examine the particular play incidents they have observed, then design new experiences to enhance and build on the child interests and ideas expressed in these incidents. Teachers also consider the personality traits and strengths of each child in the group, interpreting these in terms of a child development framework. Finally, teachers consider ways for the group as a whole to learn from and extend on the ideas and actions of individual children.

The daily plans that result from such an approach are complex, specific, and constantly in flux. And while it may be more difficult to develop these kinds of individualized plans than to teach children about "community helpers" in September and "spring" in April, High/Scope educators find that the time and energy invested in this process is amply repaid. When adults plan around the ideas and interests of children in their classrooms, they create countless "learning moments"—times when children are most receptive to internalizing new information and connecting it to their past experiences. Also, by basing their plans on children's own actions and choices, teachers give children the message that they are capable people who have some control over their learning environment. In short, by incorporating children's interests in their teaching, adults tell children that their actions have value and that others respect and respond to their abilities and ideas.

How This Book Is Organized

Each of the eight chapters that follow is organized around a general kind of play experience that is commonly seen among young children (for example, artwork, filling and emptying, or character play). Because the essence of the planning process described in this book is the development of plans based on children's observed activities, we have taken a "case history" approach. Each chapter begins with several scenarios describing the actual play experiences of children in High/Scope settings; the rest of the chapter shows how the teachers' thinking process unfolded in response to the observed play incidents. This latter part of the chapter describes the specific teaching strategies and experiences teachers planned to support children's interests, as well as some of the play activities that resulted when these plans were implemented.

Each chapter includes the following sections:

- **General teaching and interaction strategies.** These are planning and teaching ideas relating to the general topic of the chapter and the specific child interests illustrated in the opening play scenarios. Interaction strategies—techniques that are useful for communicating with children both verbally and nonverbally—are emphasized in this section.

- **Indoor and outdoor materials to add.** Listed in this section are possible materials to be added to the classroom or its outdoor play space to enable children to expand on specific interests they've expressed in their play behaviors. The suggested materials may include, for example, clothing or props that will enable children to add realism to their pretend play, books or computer programs on a particular topic, materials for representing a favorite play topic or character, or new materials that are variations of familiar materials that attract children.

- **Planning and recall experiences.** These are game-like strategies to be used at planning or recall time to hold the group's attention and playfully lead into each child's discussion of plans or experiences. Each of the strategies given in this section builds on an action or material from one of the previously described play experiences. Most of the strategies listed can be used, with slight modifications, either for planning or recall times.

- **Small-group experiences.** The suggested activities in this section are designed for one adult working with five to ten children at small-group time. The activities focus on materials or processes related to those in the opening play examples. Some of the suggested activities provide an opportunity to introduce one child's idea to other children in the group. Other experiences offer opportunities for children to try new variations of activities they particularly enjoy. Suggestions for field trips are included in this section because, even though these outings are usually planned for the group as a whole, we try to group children in small clusters throughout the outing to encourage children's active participation and to meet children's needs for adult support.

- **Large-group experiences.** This section includes ideas for whole-group movement experiences, songs, and games. Often these suggested activities provide opportunities for children to use movement or music to re-enact a favorite play interest or activity.

- **Child observations.** These are samplings of the anecdotal notes teachers recorded about the learning experiences described in the chapter. These lists of teacher observations occur twice in each chapter. The first set appears early in the chapter and relates to the play examples at the opening of the chapter; the second set appears near the end of the chapter and documents some of the child behaviors that occurred after teachers tried the teaching strategies described in the chapter. Observational notes are presented in two ways: some sets of notes are classified according to the High/Scope key experiences, others, according to the High/Scope Child Observation Record (COR). Throughout this book we have used these two curriculum tools interchangeably. This is intended to convey to teachers that either curriculum tool may be used as a child development reference, since both give developmental information that is useful in planning additional activities.

- **Adult training activities.** This last section presents adult training experiences that give teachers practice in applying the strategies presented in the chapter. These activities may be carried out by teachers working alone or with a teammate, or they may be used in group settings where adults gather for workshops or inservice training. A variety of activity formats are included.

Summary of the High/Scope Framework

The planning and teaching process described in this book takes place in the context of High/Scope learning environments. In such environments, adults and children share control of the activities that occur, and adults recognize and accept the learning power within each child. As they work with children, High/Scope-oriented adults are guided by a child development framework. In this framework the interests of the child are viewed as a vehicle for the development of basic social, physical, and cognitive abilities.

The central principles and guidelines of the High/Scope approach are summarized in the diagram at right of High/Scope's "Wheel of Learning." (For a full description of each component, see *Educating Young Children: Active Learning Practices for Preschool and Child Care Programs* by Mary Hohmann and David Weikart, High/Scope Press, 1995.) Each component of the wheel is discussed next.

Active Learning

The placement of active learning in the center of the "Wheel" indicates its central place in the High/Scope approach. High/Scope educators are guided by the belief that young children learn best when they are interacting directly with people, materials, events, and ideas. As they engage in and reflect on these direct experiences, children construct knowledge and make sense of the world around them. This process of action and reflection is called **active learning.**

All active learning experiences include the key element of **child choice.** Adults in the High/Scope approach seek to understand and promote the personal interests and intentions children are expressing through their choices. Encouraged by adults to follow their personal initiatives, children in High/Scope environments explore, ask and answer questions, solve problems that are stumbling blocks to completing their

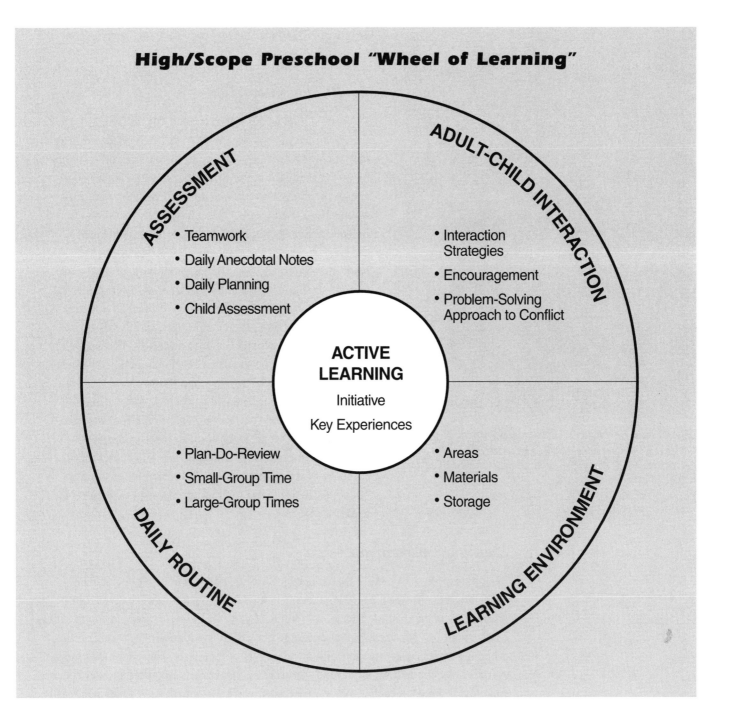

High/Scope Preschool "Wheel of Learning"

ASSESSMENT
- Teamwork
- Daily Anecdotal Notes
- Daily Planning
- Child Assessment

ADULT-CHILD INTERACTION
- Interaction Strategies
- Encouragement
- Problem-Solving Approach to Conflict

ACTIVE LEARNING
Initiative
Key Experiences

DAILY ROUTINE
- Plan-Do-Review
- Small-Group Time
- Large-Group Times

LEARNING ENVIRONMENT
- Areas
- Materials
- Storage

goals, and generate new ideas to test. As they follow their own intentions and interests in a supportive High/Scope environment, children naturally engage in **key experiences**—activities that present important learning opportunities in ten key areas of development. (A complete list of the High/Scope preschool key experiences appears on pages 8–9.)

As adults go through the process of child-oriented planning described in this book, they use High/Scope's active learning philosophy and the framework of the key

Opportunities for children to make choices are a key element of the High/Scope approach. Here Steven is carrying out his plan to use the tennis ball and the string to make a fishing rod and then to "catch some fish for dinner."

experiences to guide them as they develop plans around children's interests.

Adult-Child Interaction

The ways adults watch, listen to, and talk with children and the ways they respond to and participate in children's play have a powerful effect on how comfortable children feel in following through on their own ideas. In the High/Scope approach, adults promote **positive interactions and communications** with young children by focusing on children's individual strengths and adopting a problem-solving approach to conflict when it occurs. Throughout this book there are many "real-life" examples of children with various strengths: some children, for example, are adept at verbally communicating their wants; others, at empathizing with and supporting others; and others, in inventing creative ways to use art and building materials. The examples also illustrate how adults use a developmental perspective to identify children's strengths and then support children's further development by participating as partners in children's play or by acting as resources for children who are extending their ideas. In addition to these *examples* of positive adult-child interaction, the book also presents *guidelines* for creating such positive interactions in the "General Teaching and Interaction Strategies" section of each chapter.

Learning Environment

Designing a physical setting that supports active learning is another key element of the High/Scope framework. High/Scope active learning settings are divided into **interest areas** planned around specific kinds of play, for example, areas for house, art, block, small toy, book, computer, and sand play. Both the indoor play areas and the outdoor play space are stocked with a wide range of materials. These include practical everyday objects; natural and found materials; art materials and other open-ended supplies; all kinds of tools; "messy" materials; heavy, large materials; and small, easily handled materials. Selecting appropriate materials that will support children in following through on their interests is a key goal of the High/Scope Curriculum. The section "Indoor and Outdoor Materials to Add" in each chapter describes specific materials the teaching teams selected to build on children's observed actions.

Daily Routine

In the High/Scope approach adults maintain a balance of child- and teacher-initiated activities and provide variety and structure in the events of the day by establishing a consistent daily routine. The routine includes a plan-work-recall sequence, small- and large-group times, outside time, transition times, and times for eating and resting, if necessary.

The **plan-work-recall sequence** is the largest single block of time in the High/Scope daily routine. During the planning part of this sequence, children decide what they will do at work time and share these plans with an adult and a small group of children. During work time, the next part of the sequence, children move freely throughout the interest areas carrying out the plans they made at planning time and initiating other plans. During recall time, children return to their planning groups to discuss and reflect on what they did at work time. You will find teaching ideas to use at planning and recall times in the designated section of each chapter. For work time strategies, see the "General Teaching and Interaction Strategies" section.

Small-group time is another key component of the High/Scope daily routine. Small-group times are adult-initiated: that is, they are planned and set in motion by adults. Adults select materials for this part of the day based on their observations of children. During small-group time children freely explore and experiment with the materials provided. At **large-group time,** another adult-initiated part of the routine, all the adults and children gather as one group to participate in music and movement activities, story re-enactments, group discussions, and cooperative play and projects. In this book ideas for small-group and large-group experiences are listed in designated sections of each chapter.

Assessment

In the High/Scope Curriculum, assessment is based on daily observations of children's behaviors. Adults using the High/Scope approach believe that children's natural curiosity is a driving force behind their explorations and discoveries. When a well-designed physical environment and daily routine are in place, adults are able to observe the ways each child reacts to the materials, to the daily routine components, and to peers and teachers. As they observe, adults use the curriculum's assessment tools to help them identify children's developmentally important behaviors.

Curriculum tools for interpreting child observations

As explained above, adults implementing the High/Scope Curriculum use two basic tools as resources for understanding how children's actions relate to their developing cognitive, physical, and social skills. One tool, the High/Scope key experiences, was described previously. High/Scope's child assessment instrument, the High/Scope Child Observation Record for Ages 2½–6 (COR) is the second tool. The COR consists of 30 behavioral indicators in six child development categories that adults can use to classify and rate children's developmentally significant behaviors. The COR system of assessing children's behaviors can be used for discussion and planning purposes only or to gather data for developing formal developmental profiles of each child. (For a full explanation of how to use the COR, High/Scope COR training is recommended.)

Adults work side by side with children as they carry out their ideas and intentions.

High/Scope Preschool Key Experiences

CREATIVE REPRESENTATION

- Recognizing objects by sight, sound, touch, taste, and smell
- Imitating actions and sounds
- Relating models, pictures, and photographs to real places and things
- Pretending and role playing
- Making models out of clay, blocks, and other materials
- Drawing and painting

LANGUAGE AND LITERACY

- Talking with others about personally meaningful experiences
- Describing objects, events, and relations
- Having fun with language: listening to stories and poems, making up stories and rhymes
- Writing in various ways: drawing, scribbling, letterlike forms, invented spelling, conventional forms
- Reading in various ways: reading storybooks, signs and symbols, one's own writing
- Dictating stories

INITIATIVE AND SOCIAL RELATIONS

- Making and expressing choices, plans, and decisions
- Solving problems encountered in play
- Taking care of one's own needs
- Expressing feelings in words
- Participating in group routines
- Being sensitive to the feelings, interests, and needs of others
- Building relationships with children and adults
- Creating and experiencing collaborative play
- Dealing with social conflict

MOVEMENT

- Moving in nonlocomotor ways (anchored movement: bending, twisting, rocking, swinging one's arms)
- Moving in locomotor ways (nonanchored movement: running, jumping, hopping, skipping, marching, climbing)
- Moving with objects
- Expressing creativity in movement
- Describing movement
- Acting upon movement directions
- Feeling and expressing steady beat
- Moving in sequences to a common beat

Observing, interacting with, and planning for children require the adult's full energy and attention. Each teaching team must design an individual system of planning and assessment that works for them, but there are common elements to all such systems. One essential for all programs is to develop a system for gathering accurate anecdotal notes on each child. Anecdotal notes are brief capsule summaries of children's developmentally important behaviors. Teaching team members discuss and record these anecdotal notes in **daily planning sessions** that may take place before children arrive, after they leave, or during children's rest time. During these planning sessions adults share their observations, interpret these observations in terms of the High/Scope key experiences or COR framework, and decide on strategies for future interactions and activities. Many samples of teachers' anecdotal notes are presented throughout this book in the "Child Observations" sections.

MUSIC

- Moving to music
- Exploring and identifying sounds
- Exploring the singing voice
- Developing melody
- Singing songs
- Playing simple musical instruments

CLASSIFICATION

- Exploring and describing similarities, differences, and the attributes of things
- Distinguishing and describing shapes
- Sorting and matching
- Using and describing something in several ways
- Holding more than one attribute in mind at a time
- Distinguishing between "some" and "all"
- Describing characteristics something does not possess or what class it does not belong to

SERIATION

- Comparing attributes (longer/shorter, bigger/smaller)
- Arranging several things one after another in a series or pattern and describing the relationships (big/bigger/biggest, red/blue/red/blue)
- Fitting one ordered set of objects to another through trial and error (small cup–small saucer/medium cup–medium saucer/big cup–big saucer)

NUMBER

- Comparing the number of things in two sets to determine "more," "fewer," "same number"
- Arranging two sets of objects in one-to-one correspondence
- Counting objects

SPACE

- Filling and emptying
- Fitting things together and taking them apart
- Changing the shape and arrangement of objects (wrapping, twisting, stretching, stacking, enclosing)
- Observing people, places, and things from different spatial viewpoints
- Experiencing and describing positions, directions, and distances in the play space, building, and neighborhood
- Interpreting spatial relations in drawings, pictures, and photographs

TIME

- Starting and stopping an action on signal
- Experiencing and describing rates of movement
- Experiencing and comparing time intervals
- Anticipating, remembering, and describing sequences of events

© High/Scope Educational Research Foundation

Observation and anecdotal note-taking tips

To carry out this system of interest-based planning adults must make a commitment to careful observation and documentation of children's actions. Accurate notes on the details of children's play are necessary to help adults remember, discuss, and build on the actions of children.

Collecting accurate information about children is a skill acquired through practice. While your setting may use something other than the High/Scope key experiences or Child Observation Record (COR) as a resource for organizing child development information, you will still need some system of recording your observations to carry out the planning process described in this book. The following are strategies for successfully observing and documenting child information that High/Scope educators in the field have developed:

In High/Scope settings, children are encouraged to solve problems independently as they play. For example, Elyse figures out how to connect magnet balls to make a long chain, left, and Kelly finds a way to open a cheese snack, right. Teachers use anecdotal notes to capture "learning moments" like these.

1. **Record only *objective* information about children.** Describe the situation that you observe instead of recording your own interpretations of, opinions, or judgments about the behavior. Here is an example of an objective anecdotal note: "Sam cried for ten minutes after his father left today." By contrast, "After Sam's father left today, Sam was angry at his father and sad" is an opinion about the behavior, not a description of it.

2. **Post the High/Scope key experiences or Child Observation Record (COR) categories** or your own school's child development tool as a visible reminder of abilities to look for when observing children's actions and ideas.

3. **Place note pads strategically throughout the room or carry a note pad in your pocket.** Jot down brief observational notes while you work with the children. For example, "Sue, BA, podium, audience" later becomes, "At work time in the block area Sue placed a hollow block on the floor, stood on it, and sang in a high-pitched voice. She then arranged a number of chairs to face the block and asked classmates to be 'the audience.'"

4. **Keep samples of original artwork.** To document children's work with blocks and other materials that must be put away every day, **take photos.** *Date everything.*

5. **Record interactions by setting a tape recorder near children as they work.**

6. **Pick a child development category you want to watch for** (for example, how children move or communicate their ideas). Write that category at the top of several pieces of paper that you then post in strategic locations around the room. As you observe a child behavior related to that aspect of development, write down your

observation immediately on the nearest prepared sheet. After a week, check to make sure you have an anecdote to represent each child in the class, then create a new chart using a different category.

7. **Set aside a block of time for meeting with team members to discuss observations and plan future interactions.** Some members meet daily for 30 minutes before children arrive or after they leave, and other team members meet for a longer block of time once or twice a week. Select whatever system works best for you and your co-workers, and make sure to keep that time block free of other commitments or interruptions.

◎

This concludes our summary of the organization of this book and the basics of the High/Scope approach. The remaining chapters provide the teaching ideas promised in the title to this book. Each of these chapters highlights a general type of play experience that is familiar to early childhood teachers, as follows:

- Chapter 2. Artwork: Drawing, Painting, and Making Models

- Chapter 3. Pretending: Favorite Play Roles

- Chapter 4. Nature: Observing Plants, Animals, and Weather

- Chapter 5. Social Play: Exploring Feelings and Relationships

- Chapter 6. Celebrations: Experiencing Holidays and Special Events

- Chapter 7. "Messy" Materials: Pouring, Filling, Mixing, and Molding

- Chapter 8. Food-Related Play: Cooking, Eating, and Pretending

- Chapter 9. Character Play: Pooh, Piglet, and Power Rangers

As you read through the strategies and experiences suggested in each chapter it is important to remember that this book is not intended as a "cookbook" of teaching ideas; instead, the ideas suggested are illustrations of a general process of teaching and planning. Instead of using these ideas exactly as presented here, we suggest you use them as models for developing similar strategies and experiences that incorporate your own observations of individual children in your classrooms and centers.

Artwork 2

Drawing,

Painting, and

Making Models

F or the past few weeks, preschooler Rachel has been engrossed in making things with string. One of her favorite work time activities is making "traps," which she creates by attaching string to the classroom climbing structure and winding it around a closet door knob several feet away. She continues winding the string back and forth between the structure and the doorknob until she has many layers of string. Then she hangs toys from the string layers "so there will be noise if someone tries to open the door."

Rachel has also used string at the art area, creating interesting effects with paint by using pieces of string as paintbrushes. Today at work time, she finds a new use for string; she cuts three lengths of string, gets out three brightly colored wallpaper scraps, and tapes one to each piece of string. When she finishes, she takes her work to Carol, a teacher, and says, "Help me make a mobile so I can take it to Jeremy's school crib." (Rachel has a 12-week-old brother who has just joined the program's infant room, which is down the hall from the preschool room.)

◉

While riding a tricycle at outside time, Jonah accidentally backs into a small, open container of tempera paint that is on the sidewalk. The paint spills and creates an oblong puddle on the sidewalk. Jonah gets off his bike and watches as the puddle grows longer and deeper. After the paint stops flowing, he steps back, stares at the paint spill for almost a minute, then gets another small container of paint in a second color and carefully pours this color on top of the other, following the original paint puddle from end to end. He continues working in the same way as he adds three more colors to the paint spill, each time stepping back to examine his work. When he has used some of each available color he gets a paintbrush and begins mixing the colors together, using long, sweeping arm movements and leaning over carefully so his feet do not touch the paint. After mixing the colors, he begins to sway back and forth while shaking the wet paintbrush in the air. Paint spatters over the sidewalk, making tiny spots.

Jonah pauses to look at the spatters, then calls to Peter, his teacher, who is standing nearby, "Look, Peter, I can make colored raindrops on the ground." "Colored raindrops?" Peter says, walking over to Jonah. "Yes," answers Jonah. "Get a paintbrush, dip it here, and then shake," Jonah continues, demonstrating the process with hand gestures. Peter picks up a brush and follows Jonah's directions. They are joined by Tucker and Trevor. All four continue to dip, shake, and spatter until outside time is over. The next day Jonah goes back to look at his paint design, which is now dry. He gets some colored chalk and uses it to trace around the outside outline of the original artwork.

◎

It is small-group time and the teacher has brought metal shape templates, paper, and writing implements to the table. Kacey begins to sort through the shapes and chooses three: a circle, a square, and a rectangle. Then she traces around each template, combining the shapes to create a drawing of a person. She uses the circle template for the head, the square for the torso, and the rectangle for the arms and legs. When she completes her work she turns to another child and says, "I made mine a person. Now I'm going to give her clothes." She spends the remainder of small-group time and the beginning of the next day's work time creating an outfit for her person with magic markers, fabric scraps, sequins, and glue.

◎

It is the middle of work time and Victor is in the block area. He is sitting on a single block in front of a tower of eight blocks. "Vrooom, vrooom, vrooom," he says over and over. Kayla, who is working in the art area right next to the block area, shouts, "Stop that noise—it bothers me." Victor smiles, stamps his foot on the floor, and makes the sound again, louder this time.

After Victor and Kayla have been arguing for a while, April, the teacher, walks over calmly and sits on the floor between Victor and Kayla. "Kayla, it sounds like you're trying to say something to Victor," April says. Kayla faces Victor and repeats her complaint about the noise he is making. Then April turns to Victor and says, "Your noise bothers Kayla. Can you explain why your voice is loud?"

*Victor explains that he was driving his car to California when "the muffler blew out." "Your muffler blew out?" says April, "That **is** a loud problem." "I know how to fix a muffler," says Kayla. She runs and gets a plastic tube from the toy area. While Kayla works with Victor to "fix the muffler," April gets a different plastic tube, comes back to the block area, lies down on the floor, and pretends to work on the car in imitation of Kayla and Victor's movements.*

Young Artists at Work: Nurturing Children's Creativity

In environments where children are encouraged to explore art and building materials, it is not uncommon to observe examples like these of children creating things as they play. For some children, making something—a web of strings, a mobile, a drawing of a person, or a block car—is a way of communicating specific images and ideas they have stored in their minds. For other children, artistic creations arise spontaneously as an outgrowth of their exploration of materials. Jonah's sidewalk painting, for example, begins as an accident. Only after he has explored the materials for a while do his ideas for painting become more definite.

An understanding of the concepts and abilities that are emerging as children engage in artwork and model-making can help adults support the development of children's creative abilities. Preschool children learn through their senses, their actions, and their experiences with people and things. As they move from toddler-hood to the preschool years they develop the ability to form mental images of their experiences. Freed from the here and now by this newly emerging ability for mental representation, children can begin to communicate their ideas and experiences through drawing, painting, and model-making. When adults provide opportunities for children to express themselves through art and building experiences, children gradually develop control and skill in using these creative media. Children also develop a sense of personal investment in their work and gain a more thorough understanding of the ideas and experiences they are representing through art.

As you support children's artwork and model-making, keep in mind that children's early experiences in using art and building materials usually do not result in complex creations such as those produced by Kacey and Rachel. Rather than create representations that are recognizable to adults, many children, like Jonah, simply explore and experiment with materials. Other children, like Victor, use materials in a very simple way and then attach a verbal label to their creation.

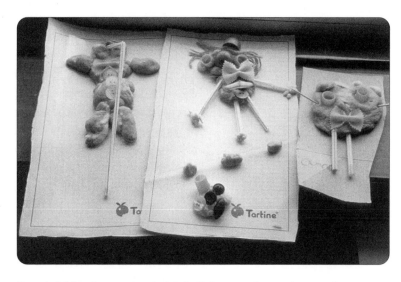

Expect children to use art materials in their own unique and personal ways.

It is important to plan ways to encourage this kind of exploratory play with drawing and model-making materials. Expect to see children layering one paint color over another (even though the result may be a muddy brown); pounding, squishing, cutting, and rolling pieces of Play-Doh and other moldable materials; lining up, balancing, rearranging, stacking, and restacking various kinds of blocks. Keep in mind the value of such exploratory actions in developing the skills children need to create and communicate in more complex ways.

Experiences with art and building materials help children develop skills and abilities in all areas. The wide range of abilities developed through such experiences

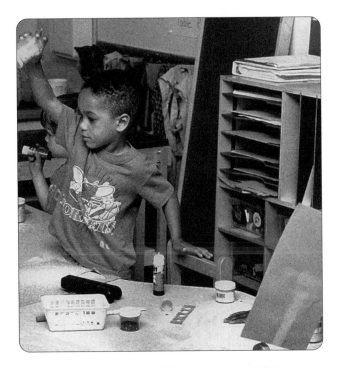

Observe and record the ways children use art materials. Some children enjoy using the materials in exploratory, physically active ways while others use them more precisely to represent specific letters, shapes, or objects.

is illustrated by the selection of "Child Observations" presented on pages 18–19. Teachers recorded these child anecdotes about the play experiences of Rachel, Jonah, Victor, and Kayla that are presented at the opening of this chapter. As the teachers discussed these anecdotal notes, they interpreted their observations according to the developmental framework provided by the High/Scope Child Observation Record (COR) assessment instrument. Each anecdote is presented with a corresponding item on the COR that identifies important abilities that are reflected in the child's behavior. As they planned subsequent strategies and experiences for these children, the teachers considered how to offer opportunities for children to continue to develop these abilities in the context of their interests.

Supporting Children's Interest in Drawing, Painting, and Making Models

Creativity, problem solving, personal expression, and decision-making—these are the cornerstones of a "partnership" approach to art and model-making in the early childhood classroom. High/Scope's partnership approach contrasts with teacher-directed approaches in which the adult plans specific art and model-making projects and then supervises children in completing them. In High/Scope's process-oriented approach, the adult's role is not to direct children but to encourage and participate in their work, observing and imitating children and occasionally modeling new ideas and techniques that children may not have considered on their own.

The following are strategies the teachers developed to support the interests expressed by Rachel, Jonah, Kacey, Victor, Kayla, and their classmates in their drawing, painting, and model-making. Their ideas incorporate *general strategies* that work with all kinds of art-related play and *specific strategies* that relate to these children's interests in working with string, spatter painting, clothing design, and car building/repairing.

General Teaching and Interaction Strategies

✔ **Turn those times when children ask for your help into occasions for learning and problem solving.** Rachel's teacher, for example, recognized that Rachel had been working independently to make a mobile for her brother until she asked for help in completing her plan. The teacher responded by giving Rachel the support she needed to complete the project herself; the teacher avoided "taking over." When

Rachel said, "Help me make a mobile so I can take it to Jeremy's school crib," the adult might have said something like "Oh, sure, tomorrow I'll bring a plastic coat hanger and you can tie your papers on that." Instead, the adult made a response that encouraged Rachel to think about the materials that might be available for completing her project. "A mobile—you want to make a mobile?" the adult said, pausing for a moment and waiting for additional information about Rachel's understanding of what was needed. When Rachel said, "Yeah, that stuff that hangs over his head," the teacher then said, "So, you need these to hang from some-thing?" "Yes," Rachel answered, "You find it." After the teacher suggested that they look through the room together to find something that might work, Rachel decided to tie the strings to a paper towel tube.

✔ **Wait until you're invited by the child to discuss or participate in the child's explorations,** even though you may be strongly tempted to get involved earlier. Peter, Jonah's teacher, could have said many things about what Jonah was experiencing as he experimented with the spilled paint on the sidewalk. Comments like "The paint looks like it's running," "Blue and red make purple," and "I wonder what would happen if you used a paintbrush," are all possible responses. Some adults would argue that comments like these might have encour-aged Jonah to think about and learn something from his experience. In addition, joining immediately in Jonah's play might have been a fun activity for Peter, who espe-cially enjoyed painting and other art activities. Nevertheless, Peter did not say or do any of these things because, in the High/Scope approach, we recommend that teaching adults wait for an invitation to converse with children or enter their play. We urge adults to first watch and listen to children and then to base their interaction strategies and comments on the specific things they observe children doing. This is the approach that Peter used. Because he resisted the temptation to go to Jonah right away, Peter had the oppor-tunity to observe the ways Jonah was using the paint. Peter's willingness to let Jonah experiment on his own also gave Jonah the opportunity to discover a way to use his whole body to make spatter marks on the sidewalk. Later, when Peter did join Jonah, he participated on Jonah's terms and used the painting materials the way Jonah did.

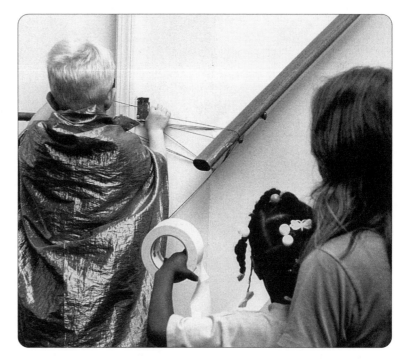

Watch and wait to be invited into children's work, as this teacher does.

✔ **Support and build on children's play ideas, staying within the context set by the child.** The fact that Victor's actual car design was very simple did not keep him

Child Observations

INITIATIVE

TEACHER'S ANECDOTAL NOTES

*HIGH/SCOPE COR ITEM AND LEVEL**

At outside time Jonah made a design out of a paint spill created when his bicycle knocked over a paint container. He added four new colors to the spill, carefully pouring paint from left to right.

A. Expressing choices: (2) Child indicates a desired activity or place of activity by saying a word, pointing, or some other action.

At work time Rachel used Scotch tape to attach one wallpaper scrap to each of three pieces of string.

B. Solving problems: (3) Child uses one method to try and solve a problem, but if unsuccessful, gives up after one or two tries.

At small-group time Kacey traced around square, triangular, and rectangular templates to make "a person." The next day at work time she took her person to the art area and made clothing for it by using markers, fabric scraps, sequins, and glue.

C. Engaging in complex play: (4) Child, acting alone, carries out complex and varied sequences of activities.

SOCIAL RELATIONS

TEACHER'S ANECDOTAL NOTES

HIGH/SCOPE COR ITEM AND LEVEL

At work time Rachel brought her artwork (three brightly colored scraps of wallpaper attached to three pieces of string) to Carol [her teacher] and said, "Help me make a mobile so I can take it to Jeremy's school crib."

E. Relating to adults: (3) Child initiates interactions with familiar adults.

After Kayla offered to help Victor fix his car's muffler at work time, they worked together for 15 minutes using plastic tubes from the toy area.

F. Relating to other children: (4) Child sustains interactions with other children.

At work time, when Victor was making loud "vrooom, vrooom" sounds, Kayla said, "Stop that noise—it bothers me."

H. Engaging in social problem solving: (4) Child sometimes attempts to solve problems with other children independently, by negotiation or other socially acceptable means.

CREATIVE REPRESENTATION

TEACHER'S ANECDOTAL NOTES

HIGH/SCOPE COR ITEM AND LEVEL

At small-group time and the next day at work time, Kacey made a person with a head, body, arms, and legs. She then dressed her person in fabric scrap clothing with sequins around the edges of the clothing.

J. Making and building: (5) Child uses materials to make or build things with at least three details represented.

At outside time Jonah created a design on the sidewalk by pouring paint colors on top of each other. He then mixed them together with a brush and used the brush to flick paint spots on the ground as he swayed back and forth.

K. Drawing and painting: (2) Child explores drawing and painting materials.

TEACHER'S ANECDOTAL NOTES	*HIGH/SCOPE COR ITEM AND LEVEL*
At work time Victor and Kayla used plastic tube toys as tools while pretending to fix Victor's noisy muffler.	L. Pretending: (4) Child engages in cooperative pretend play with another child.

MUSIC AND MOVEMENT

TEACHER'S ANECDOTAL NOTES	*HIGH/SCOPE COR ITEM AND LEVEL*
Rachel pulled three pieces of tape from the dispenser and used them to connect string to paper.	N. Exhibiting manual coordination: (4) Child manipulates small objects with precision.
At outside time Jonah called Peter over and explained how to make colored raindrops on the sidewalk, using actions to demonstrate as he spoke the words "Get a paintbrush, dip it here, and then shake."	P. Following music and movement directions: (5) Child describes and carries out movement sequences.

LANGUAGE AND LITERACY

TEACHER'S ANECDOTAL NOTES	*HIGH/SCOPE COR ITEM AND LEVEL*
After Kayla told Victor the noises he was making were too loud and April [a teacher] repeated Kayla's words to Victor, he explained that he was driving to California and his "muffler blew out."	Q. Understanding speech: (3) Child responds to simple, direct, conversational sentences.
At outside time Jonah told Peter, "I made colored raindrops on the ground."	R. Speaking: (2) Child uses simple sentences of more than two words.

LOGIC AND MATHEMATICS

TEACHER'S ANECDOTAL NOTES	*HIGH/SCOPE COR ITEM AND LEVEL*
At work time Rachel got three of each of the following items: wallpaper scraps, pieces of string, and pieces of tape. She then used the tape to attach one piece of string to each of the paper scraps.	BB. Counting objects: (3) Child correctly counts up to three objects.
After building a "trap" out of string and hanging objects at work time, Rachel explained its purpose: "so there will be noise if someone tries to open the door."	DD. Describing sequence and time: (2) Child plans or anticipates the next event in a sequence.

*The COR item (lettered) is a general label for a type of child behavior described in the teacher's anecdotal note. The COR level (the numbered statement that follows) is a more specific description of the child's behavior indicating the child's developmental level within that item.

from giving a relatively elaborate *verbal* description of his project. His discussion of his "broken muffler" showed an understanding of cars that was not apparent in the simple block structure he had built to represent a car. Realizing that verbal representation was an important part of Victor's project, the teacher repeated Victor's words and acknowledged that a broken muffler "is a loud problem." This comment seemed to spark Kayla's idea about fixing the muffler.

✔ **Examine the ways you communicate with children about their art and model-making creations, so as to avoid complimenting or praising children.** For example, Kacey's teacher might have said, "Kacey, what a lovely clothing design you made for your person. She's pretty." Victor's teacher might have said, "Victor, that's a really neat block tower you made." While such statements might have been true, they would have done little to encourage a dialogue or further interaction. Simply watching a child at work, as Kacey's teacher did, or making a comment that builds on the child's own description of his project, as Victor's teacher did, is more likely to result in a dialogue that encourages children to reflect on their work.

✔ **As you consider what uses of materials are appropriate, take the perspective of the child who is discovering and exploring materials.** As an adult it is easy to fall into the trap of viewing a painting experiment like Jonah's as a "waste of paint." It's important to keep in mind, however, that young children who are exploring and developing new skills may often use what seems like an excess of materials. If you continue to worry about children wasting materials, fill your paint or glue continuers only part way instead of interrupting children's explorations with lessons on using too much or many of the materials. Or, provide additional, inexpensive materials children can use for pouring and mixing, for example, water and cornstarch.

Indoor and Outdoor Materials to Add

Stringing and tying

1 If children, like Rachel, have shown an interest in working with mobiles, stock the art area with materials that children can safely hang things from. These might include plastic coat hangers, tree branches, wooden dowels in various thicknesses, cardboard toilet paper or paper towel tubes, and plastic or wooden Popsicle sticks or tongue depressors.

2 To support children's interest in tying and stringing, add a simple loom and weaving materials to your center. In one classroom a parent volunteer made a simple free-standing wooden frame (about 4 feet by 6 feet) for weaving. Teachers tied yarn strings from the top dowel to the bottom dowel all the way across the loom. They also provided containers filled with yarn, paper strips of varying lengths and thicknesses, pieces of colored paper with holes punched in them, natural items like

twigs and long grasses, balls of twine, and rope. Children wove and unwove various designs on the loom using the materials provided and adding other materials found outdoors or in other parts of the classroom.

Painting

3 When you observe children discovering creative ways to paint, add additional materials to encourage further experimentation. To encourage Jonah's interest in spatter-painting and mixing colors, the teachers made additional painting materials available in the art area, or, when appropriate, outdoors on the playground. The materials included toothbrushes and netting or screening stretched over wooden frames; fly swatters and shallow containers of paint; coffee filters, plastic eyedroppers, and food colorings; and plastic squeeze containers partially full of paint. The teachers added one set of materials at a time, introducing each group of materials first at small-group time (see strategies 3, 4, and 5, "Small-Group Experiences," pages 25–26) before making them available at work time or outside time.

4 To support children's interest in noticing and exploring different paint textures, provide a range of painting tools, painting surfaces, and paints. For example, Jonah's teachers added a selection of brushes, combs, toothbrushes, cotton swabs, and cotton balls to the art area for children to use as painting tools. They also provided a variety of painting surfaces—the table, canvas, Plexiglas, cellophane, boxes, and various kinds of paper. They also made available special paints to which various materials had been added—sugar, salt, evaporated milk, coffee grounds, soap flakes, and glitter—to create textured effects. The teachers introduced these materials in a series of small-group times (see "Small-Group Experiences," strategy 6, page 26) before they made them available in the classroom.

Offering both toothbrushes and ordinary paintbrushes with the painting materials gives these children an opportunity to experiment with painting in new ways.

5 Add books like *Color Farm* by Lois Ehlert and *My Head Is Full of Colors* by Catherine Friend to the book area. If you have computers, children enjoy coloring and drawing programs such as *Kid Pix* (Broderbund) and *Dinosaurs Are Forever* (Merit).

Clothing design

6 To build on children's interest in clothing design, ask a local fabric store to lend or donate a child-size mannequin and large, flowing fabric scraps to wrap around

*The interest children showed in the book **Color Farm,** which includes cut-outs of various shapes, inspires the teacher to provide metal shape templates for a small-group experience, left. At work time the day after the small-group time in which children traced around metal shape templates, Kacey, right, finds other interesting things to trace around.*

it. To enable children to complete the outfits they design, set out dress-up accessories such as used jewelry, scarves, hats, and gloves. The children may also be interested in using these materials to create outfits for themselves, their baby dolls, and stuffed animals.

7 Make sewing materials available: additional fabric scraps, plastic embroidery needles, yarn, and thread.

8 Put paper dolls with paper clothing in the toy area. Select clothing that can be used for a variety of make-believe occasions (for dress-up, sporting events, going to work, and so forth).

Car building/repairing

9 When children, like Victor and Kayla, express an interest in car building and repairs, look for real car parts and accessories to add to the center. At the request of Victor's teachers, a local body shop donated a steering wheel and a gear-shift stick to his preschool. To add to these materials, Victor's teachers also gathered several sets of car keys, pairs of old driving gloves, screwdrivers, wrenches, fan belts, and flashlights (which children used to shine under the "cars" during repairs).

10 Add a variety of scrap materials to the construction area to support three-dimensional car building. For example, include sturdy cardboard boxes, plastic lids from milk containers, bottle caps, pipe cleaners, nuts and bolts, decals, wood pieces, hammers, nails, and glue.

11 Make sure the building sets you have available in the toy area include wheels, axles, and other auto parts so they can be used to construct cars and other kinds of vehicles.

12 If possible, obtain a real used car for your playground. One very ambitious teaching team had an old car body hauled to their school playground and embedded

the bottom of the frame in the ground to stabilize it. Children spent hours driving the "convertible" and enjoyed washing, drying, "repairing," and even "repainting" the car.

Planning and Recall Experiences

Stringing and tying

1 To build on children's interest in making traps from string, tie some toys to a string, arranging them so that shaking the string makes a noise. While the other children cover their eyes, the person who is sharing plans or experiences carries the "trap" to the chosen interest area and shakes it. The others then try to guess the origin of the sound. Once the correct interest area has been named, the child discusses his or her ideas.

2 Make a mobile of the interest area symbols (or objects from the interest areas) and hang it a few feet above the floor. Ask individual children to take turns lying down under the mobile, touching the symbol or object for the area they will work in or have worked in, and discussing their plans or experiences.

3 Give children materials to make their own work time mobiles: hangers or dowels, string, paper area symbols, objects from the interest areas, and art materials. On their mobiles children hang the symbol(s) for or object(s) from the interest areas they plan to work in or have worked in that day.

When children's pretending revolves around cars, trucks, and other vehicles, add real vehicle parts to the classroom (such as this steering wheel). This will encourage children to add details to their pretend play.

Painting

4 Bring a clear plastic container filled with water to the table, along with three squeeze-bottles filled with different-colored paints. As each child describes work time plans or experiences, he or she chooses a paint to squeeze into the clear water. Encourage children to observe the ways the added color changes the water.

Clothing design

5 If children have been making dressed-up paper people, ask a child's permission to use his or her creation as a prop for planning or recalling. (Another option is to

make your own person similar to the ones you have seen children making.) The child holds the paper person and pretends to tell it his or her plans or experiences.

6 Cut out the figure of a person from heavy cardboard. Make several one-piece paper outfits shaped like the person's body, marking each outfit with an area symbol. Attach pieces of Velcro to the figure and the paper outfits so that children can fasten the clothes to the person. To indicate where they plan to work or have worked, children attach the corresponding outfit to the person and then describe their plans or experiences.

7 Bring dress-up props (such as a hat, a piece of jewelry, a scarf, and a pair of gloves) to the planning/recall table. The child chooses one prop to wear while sharing his or her work time ideas.

Car building/repairing

8 Bring a car part or accessory (steering wheel, gear-shift stick, or driving gloves) to the planning/recall table. Each child holds the prop while sharing his or her work time ideas.

9 Make a car out of Bristle Blocks, Legos, or other small building toys. Children take turns sharing their plans or experiences and then choosing the next person to plan or recall by "driving" the car over to that person.

The day after a work time in which children were heavily involved in pretending to build and repair cars, teachers have set up a "planning road" marked with symbols of the interest areas. To indicate where they plan to work, children move small cars to the symbols designating their chosen area.

Small-Group Experiences

Stringing and tying

1 When a child shows a strong interest in making particular kinds of art projects at work time, follow up on this interest by providing similar materials for the small group to experiment with. Then watch as children's efforts unfold. For example, the day after Rachel initiated her mobile-making project, the teacher set out mobile-making materials (paper, markers, hole punches, string, dowels, yarn, and sticks) for small-group time. The teacher opened the activity by reminding children of the present Rachel made for her brother Jeremy: "Today at small group we'll be using materials like the ones Rachel used to make a crib toy for Jeremy. Let's see what you can do with them."

2 Take your group outside and provide yarn, string, crepe paper streamers, and other materials for a tying and

weaving experience. When the teachers tried this strategy with one small group in Rachel's classroom, the children wove the materials through the openings in the metal chain-link fence; on the next day, the teachers watched and participated as children in the other small group roamed the yard, tying the materials to the poles of the swing set; attaching them to tree trunks; and winding them, Maypole fashion, around the timbers of the climbing structure.

Painting

3 When children discover interesting painting effects during their activities at work time or outside time, provide opportunities for them to re-create these effects with a different set of materials. To help children re-create the spatter-painting effect that fascinated Jonah, his teachers planned an outdoor small-group time in which children worked with fly swatters and paint set out in wide, shallow containers. Children enjoyed making paint prints with the fly swatters on the sidewalk, as well as shaking the fly swatters to make spatter-paint effects. A possible variation of this strategy is to provide screening or netting stretched over a frame, toothbrushes, paint, and paper. Children dip the toothbrushes in the paint and brush them across the screening or netting, creating interesting paint marks on the paper or pavement below the screen.

To support children's interest in combining and mixing colors, teachers planned a small-group experience in which children "painted" on coffee filters using eyedroppers, food coloring, and water.

4 Plan a series of small-group experiences to enable children to experiment with mixing colors. For one day's activity, use food colorings to make colored water and put several different colors in clear containers. Provide plastic eyedroppers and

coffee filters for children to use with the colored waters. Encourage children to drop the colored water onto the coffee filters and watch what happens when the colors spread through the filter and mix with each other. On another day, set out small containers of liquid laundry starch, paintbrushes, and several colors of tissue paper cut into different small shapes. Observe children's reactions as they experiment with "painting" the tissue pieces onto other pieces of tissue; they will discover interesting effects as the colors blend and the paper stiffens from the starch.

5 Fill plastic mustard and ketchup bottles with paint, lay a large piece of paper on the floor (or on an outdoor surface), and encourage children to make a squirt-painting. You can also try this on another day at the sand and water table: line the bottom of the water table with newspaper and put white paper over it for the painting surface.

6 To encourage children to notice and explore varied paint textures and painting effects, introduce new painting tools, painting surfaces, and types of paint in a series of small-group times conducted over several days; then add the materials to the art area. For use as painting tools, the materials could include a range of brushes, cotton swabs, and cotton balls, and for painting surfaces, various kinds of paper, the table, canvas, and Plexiglas. In addition, the following materials may be added to paints to change the texture produced: sugar, salt, evaporated milk, coffee grounds, soap flakes, and glitter.

Clothing design

7 Ask parents to donate old pairs of shoes. When you have one pair for each child, make the shoes available at small-group time along with glue, sequins, glitter, and paint. Ask children to "redesign the shoes to make a new pair." Later, have the children dance in the shoes they have made (see "Large-Group Experiences," strategy 4, page 28.

Car building/repairing

8 Arrange to visit a local service station. Talk to the owner beforehand to explain children's need for active involvement; if possible, arrange for children to look under the hoods of cars that are being repaired, see the undersides of cars that are on hydraulic lifts, and physically experience some of the materials (for example, hold a few tools, examine some new car parts, feel the outside edges of tires, or sit inside a tire).

9 Provide put-together-take-apart materials, such as Bristle Blocks, Legos, or Duplos, for children to use in creating their own models of cars and other objects. Observe and record which children use the materials in exploratory ways and which use them to make models that they identify as specific objects. Consider these observations in terms of children's representational abilities.

Large-Group Experiences

Stringing and tying

1 Make a string creation for each child by attaching brightly colored pieces of paper to a piece of string or use string creations children have made themselves at a previous small-group time (make some extras for those children who were absent that day or do not want to use their own creation). Put on a musical selection (such as "Yankee Doodle" from Volume 2 of the *Rhythmically Moving* recording series from High/Scope Press) and ask children to "dance" their string creations (as if they were puppets) on the floor.

Painting

2 Make up a song about ways you have observed children using paint to the tune of "Johnny Works With One Hammer." Encourage children to make the appropriate painting motions as they sing. For example:

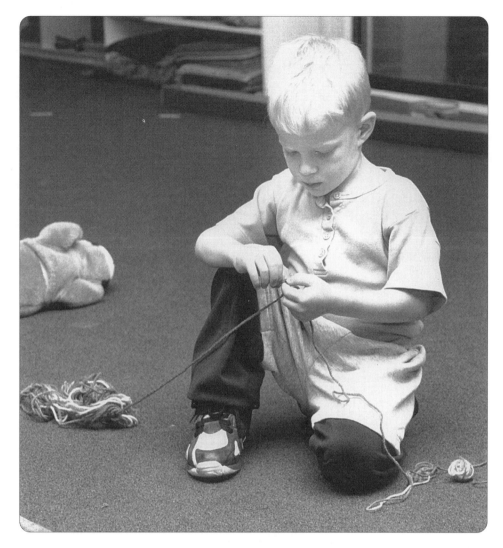

A tiny knot in a piece of string provides an interesting problem for Brendan to solve as he makes a string "puppet." Later Brendan will dance with his "puppet" at large-group time.

> Jonah sways with one paintbrush,
> One paintbrush, one paintbrush.
> Jonah sways with one paintbrush,
> Now he sways with two.

3 Build on children's spatter-painting experiences by making "colored raindrops" out of heavy pieces of colored oak tag paper. Scatter them around the floor, so there are more than the number of children in your class. Play a musical selection (for example, "Blackberry Quadrille" from Volume 2, *Rhythmically Moving*) and ask children to dance around the raindrops, and when the music stops, to run and stand on a raindrop.

Clothing design

4 Set out the shoes children decorated at a previous day's small-group time (see "Small-Group Experiences," strategy 7, page 26). Have children try on their pair. Then play some dance music (for example, "Alley Cat" from Volume 3, *Rhythmically Moving*), and have them dance while wearing their creations.

Car building/repairing

5 Pick two distinct sounds, such as a whistle blowing and a maraca shaking. Ask children to pretend they are cars with noisy mufflers driving around the large-group space. Blow the whistle to signal them to start "driving." Then ask them to pretend their mufflers are repaired, and shake the maraca to signal them to make the motions and sounds of a car that is fixed. Alternate the signals at a slow pace, watching how children respond.

6 Make up a song about driving, building, or repairing cars to the tune of "Here We Go Looby Loo," asking children to suggest ideas for new verses. For example:

> Here we go looby loo,
> Here we go looby lie.
> Here we go looby loo,
> All on a Saturday night. [Children skip around the circle.]

> I put the key inside [act out the motion],
> I put the key inside.
> I put the key inside.
> All on a Saturday night.
> [Repeat first verse.]

Other verses might include, "It makes a lot of noise," "I drive it really fast," "I drive it very slowly," "I take it to the station," "I got the muffler fixed," and "I put the gas inside."

What We Learned From Our Observations of Children

After the teaching strategies suggested in this chapter were tried, teachers recorded anecdotes describing what they learned about the children in their classrooms. They discussed and interpreted the anecdotes in terms of the developmental framework provided by the High/Scope key experiences. Some of these anecdotes, grouped according to the key experience categories, are presented in "Child Observations" (see pages 30–31). These anecdotes illustrate the wide range of learning experiences that occur as children express their creativity through drawing, painting, and model-making. Note that all the key experience categories are included in the teachers' observations and that the learning experiences recorded occurred throughout the classroom and the daily routine. By responding to the specific child interests they observed, teachers inspired more creativity in children.

Adult Training Activities

This training experience is designed to stimulate discussion about the benefits of adult participation in children's artwork and model-making, with the adult using a "partnership" approach and following the child's lead.

1. Give participants the following directions:
   For this role-play activity, you will need two "adult team members" and several "children." Working with your team-teaching partner, take turns role-playing two distinctly different adult roles for interacting with children as they work with art or model-making materials. When you are done role-playing, compare the reactions children might have had to your different interaction styles, noting possible child reactions. The two roles are as follows:

The teaching team planned this large-group activity around one child's interest in working with string, yarn, and other tying and weaving materials. The teachers have provided long streamers tied to sticks and encourage children to move with them to the music.

   Role 1: Sit near children as they work. Without starting a conversation with children, imitate what you observe children doing. Use similar materials in similar ways; for example, if you are sitting at the art table near children who are gluing sequins and glitter on paper, do the same. WAIT for a child to ask you a specific question or make a comment about his work; then you may begin talking, but stay with the topic the child has introduced.

   Role 2: Enter children's activities by asking questions or praising the work they are doing. Some examples of things you might say: "Mark, what are you making with the blocks today?" "Trey, you're doing a great job drawing those cartoon characters. What words would you like me to write on your paper?"

   Child Reactions to Role 1:

   Child Reactions to Role 2:

2. Discuss the following questions with the group as a whole:
   What did you learn about individual children and their choices in each role play?
   How long did the interactions last in each role play?
   What are the advantages or disadvantages of each adult role?

Child Observations

CREATIVE REPRESENTATION

"This smells like my Mom's morning coffee," Carleen said to Megan as she used paint mixed with coffee grounds at small-group time.

At work time Julia wrapped the flowing fabric around her body, put on high-heeled shoes, and said, "I'm Cinderella going to the ball."

During work time at the construction area, Micah took a piece of wood and used the hammer to nail a bottle cap to each side of it. She then lay on the floor with her model, pushing it back and forth and saying "Red light, stop. Green light, go."

LANGUAGE AND LITERACY

At large-group time, as the class sang a made-up version of "Looby Loo" [with car-oriented verses], Brian added this verse: "I put my foot on the brake."

*At greeting circle Fred brought the book **Color Farm** to Kacey and said, "Read this to me. It has shapes like from your person."*

*At work time Micah used the markers to add scribble lines to the car she had made from wood scraps. At recall time she pointed to the lines and said, "This says **minivan.**"*

*After helping Victor pretend to fix his muffler at work time, Kayla brought a piece of paper and a marker to April [a teacher] and said, "Write **Kayla's garage.**"*

INITIATIVE AND SOCIAL RELATIONS

"Pass me the red paint," said Tanuka to Sue at small-group time. *"I want to mix it with green to see what happens."*

"This is a fun way to paint—more than the easel," said Audie to Carol [a teacher] while painting with fly swatters at small-group time.

After describing his work time plan, Mark said, "I'm excited about squeezing the purple paint, because purple is my favorite color."

MOVEMENT

"I can't make the wheel go around and around and around like a real car," said Donald as he moved his hands in a circular pattern. (He was referring to the plastic lid he had glued on the car model he was making at small-group time.)

At work time, while sitting on a block structure and holding onto the steering wheel, Athi bounced up and down and told Madison (who was seated behind him), "You have to bounce like me because this is a bumpy road."

At large-group time, as children were dancing while wearing the shoes they had decorated, Mark (who was wearing high-heeled shoes) said, "It's hard to dance in these shoes."

MUSIC

At recall time Ilana shouted, "I think she's in the book area," having located Rachel by the sound of her dangling bells.

At small-group time Victor rubbed his toothbrush back and forth across the metal screening and said, "Listen, I'm making a song."

CLASSIFICATION

"I'll use the toothbrush to paint because the fly swatter is too big," Trey explained to his group at planning time.

When Carol [a teacher] set out fly swatters at small-group time, Elena said, "Some of the time we use these to squash bugs."

"Rachel made a mobile but I don't have a baby—so I'm just going to make a picture," said Samuel when provided with mobile-making materials at small-group time.

SERIATION

"Blue is dripping the longest," squealed Alana as she watched paint drip down her picture at work time.

"I need bigger wheels to hammer on my car, 'cause it's a race car," said Victor as he worked with wood and bottle caps at the construction area at work time.

"I put many sequins on my person's dress because it looks prettiest that way," Kacey told Emma at work time.

NUMBER

"Hey, everybody got two," commented Fred at small-group time as children decorated pairs of shoes.

After helping Victor fix his pretend muffler at work time, Kayla said, "You owe me thirty-seven hundred."

SPACE

Theresa took a streamer and wove it in and out of the openings in a chain-link fence at small-group time. After she finished weaving with one streamer, she got a second one and commented, "Look, I made a long color line."

After the trip to the gas station, at work time Maria got three cylinder blocks, stacked them on top of one another, and placed a toy car on top of the stack.

TIME

"It will take a long, long, long, time to dry because I used all the colors," said Megan as she hung up her picture at work time.

Maria made a plan to "play eyedropper-painting like yesterday at small-group time."

Pretending 3

Favorite

Play Roles

Four-year-old Sue stands on top of a hollow block in the middle of the block area rug. She carefully straightens her body, clasps her hands in front of her stomach, and begins to sing unrecognizable words in a high-pitched voice. A few minutes later, Sue arranges a semicircle of chairs to face her single-block stage. Then she calls out to nearby classmates, "Take your seats. You be the audience." After some of the children do sit down, Sue returns to her podium, repeats her earlier actions, and begins to sing again, occasionally pausing to tell children who try to leave, "Sit back down—I'm not finished." When she finishes singing, Sue tells her audience to clap, which they do. At recall time she explains to her group that she was playing "opera" and that first she had to "practice my piece."

⊚

During naptime 3-year-old Tanuka, who has chosen not to sleep, sits quietly on her cot playing with several small toy vehicles—three cars, a steam roller, a digger, and a dump truck. Working systematically down her cot, one section at a time, she takes the digger and pushes it back and forth over the fabric. She then wheels the digger to the dump truck and spills the imaginary contents into it. When she is finished digging and dumping in one section, Tanuka pushes the steam roller very slowly over the same patch of fabric. Only then does she turn to an adult to request another vehicle, "the school bus," so she can "drive the children to school on the fresh road."

⊚

At outside time four children form a small circle under a climbing structure. As an adult approaches, the children chase after her, grab her hands, pull her back to the climbing structure, and tell her she is "under arrest." The game continues for the remainder of outside time, with the adult repeatedly escaping from the "jail" and the children recapturing her each time.

Each day at planning time for several weeks, Mark says his plan is to "be a horse." Then, at work time, Mark gets down on all fours, crawls around the room and under tables, and raises his "front paws" to whinny at anyone in his path. Soon the teachers observe other children in the class pretending to be dogs, cats, and birds.

Play-Acting: A Channel for Experience and Imagination

Young children are imaginative, and play scenarios like these are typical of the ways adults observe children using their imaginations. As they act out such scenarios, children re-live their own experiences, imitate the actions of important people in their lives, and wrestle with their fears about the world around them. Given a supportive setting, children often surprise their teachers with their ability to remember details, work through problem situations, and combine materials in new and creative ways as they pretend.

Mark carries out his plan "to be a horse," left, and Frances soon follows suit, right.

In addition to illustrating the general processes at work as children act out play roles, these anecdotes highlight some common themes in children's pretend play: performances, vehicles, prisons, and animals. In discussing ways to support children's pretend play, we'll show how adults use the details of such child-created scenarios, in concert with their understanding of child development, to devise specific strategies for enhancing children's learning experiences.

Depending on their attitudes and the interaction strategies they use, adults may either squelch or encourage children's interest in pretending and role-playing. It is not unusual for adults to respond to children's pretending by objecting to the content or timing of the play scenario: for example, telling Sue it's impolite to demand an audience, warning Tanuka that naptime is the time when eyes are closed and toys are not a choice, informing the pretend jailers, "I don't want to be arrested because I didn't do anything wrong," or telling Mark, "I would rather children act like people, not animals."

"Now I need a barn to go to sleep," says Frances, after wandering around on all fours for most of work time.

Such comments can discourage children's inventiveness. On the other hand, when adults encourage children to play imaginatively, even when their dramas are messy, loud, or otherwise out of step with adult notions of appropriate behavior, they find that children develop many important cognitive, social, and emotional skills as they pretend. When the teaching team sat down to discuss and record their observations about the above play scenarios, using the High/Scope Child Observation Record (COR) as a resource, they noted a number of observations about the developing abilities of individual children. See the box on pages 36–37 for some of the teachers' anecdotal notes and the COR items and levels they selected to match each anecdote.

Supporting Children's Pretending and Role Play

As with any other ability that children are acquiring, you can help children develop their capacity for pretending and role play by building on their actions, taking into consideration their individual interests and developmental levels. As the teachers discussed and recorded the above observations of children's pretend play, they developed the following strategies to support this play. Many of these strategies are directly tied to the interests children

"Sit down right here. This is the jail," says Trey, as he and Glen use plastic Tinkertoy sticks to lock their teacher inside.

CHILD OBSERVATIONS

INITIATIVE

TEACHER'S ANECDOTAL NOTES	HIGH/SCOPE COR ITEM AND LEVEL
Mark's plan for the day was "to be a horse."	A. Expressing choices: (3) Child indicates desired activity, place of activity, materials, or playmates with a short sentence.
At work time in the block area Sue placed the hollow block on the floor, stood on it, and sang in a high-pitched voice. She then arranged a number of chairs to face her block and asked classmates to be "the audience."	C. Engaging in complex play: (3) Child, acting alone, uses materials or organizes active play involving two or more steps.
At naptime Tanuka used the toy vehicles—a digger, a dump truck, and a steam roller—to make a "fresh road" on a section of her cot. First she pushed the digger over the area, then pretended to empty the contents, then smoothed the area with the steam roller. She repeated these actions with several other sections of the cot.	C. Engaging in complex play: (3) Child, acting alone, uses materials or organizes active play involving two or more steps.

SOCIAL RELATIONS

TEACHER'S ANECDOTAL NOTES	HIGH/SCOPE COR ITEM AND LEVEL
At work time as Sue stood on the block, singing, Brian left his chair in the "audience." Sue said, "Sit back down—I'm not finished," and Brian sat down.	H. Engaging in social problem solving: (4) Child sometimes attempts to solve problems with other children independently, by negotiation or other socially acceptable means.
At work time, when Sue finished singing, she told Brian to clap and he did.	F. Relating to other children: (2) Child responds when other children initiate interactions.

expressed in performances, vehicles, prison-related play, and animal impersonations, but teachers may adapt the strategies to other themes they observe in children's pretending. The key to successful support of children's pretend play is careful child observation to determine children's individual patterns of interests and abilities.

General Teaching and Interaction Strategies

✔ **Play side by side with the children using the same materials or actions you see them using.** When Mark crawled around the classroom on all fours, one of the adults crawled after him, pausing to stop when Mark did, imitating Mark's whinnying sound, and breaking into a gallop when Mark did. When Sue set up her chairs and invited her classmates to watch the performance, an adult asked if

CREATIVE REPRESENTATION

TEACHER'S ANECDOTAL NOTES	HIGH/SCOPE COR ITEM AND LEVEL
At recall time Sue explained that her action of standing on a hollow block and clasping her hands in front of her stomach at work time was playing "opera" and practicing her piece.	J. Making and building: (4) Child uses materials to make a simple representation and says or demonstrates what it is.
At naptime Tanuka pushed the digger on her cot and emptied the imaginary contents into the dump truck. Then she slowly pushed the steam roller over the same surface.	L. Pretending: (2) Child uses one object to stand for another or uses actions or sounds to pretend.
At work time Mark crawled around the room and under tables, raising his "front paws" and whinnying at anyone in his path.	L. Pretending: (3) Child assumes the role of someone or something else, or talks in a language appropriate to the assumed role.

LANGUAGE AND LITERACY

TEACHER'S ANECDOTAL NOTES	HIGH/SCOPE COR ITEM AND LEVEL
At work time when Sue called out to children, "Take your seats—you be the audience," Ruthie was the first to sit down.	Q. Understanding speech: (2) Child follows single directions.
At outside time, Michael chased his teacher, grabbed her hands, and said, "You're under arrest."	R. Speaking: (2) Child uses simple sentences of more than two words.
Tanuka turned to Stephanie at naptime and said, "I want the school bus so I can drive the children to school on the fresh road."	R. Speaking: (3) Child uses sentences that include two or more separate ideas.

there was room for one more in her audience. The adult sat quietly and watched Sue, paying close attention to her singing and gestures.

✔ **Play the role the children suggest to you.** As Carleen and Megan pretended to be kittens, a teacher lay on the floor next to them making meowing and purring sounds. Not long afterwards, the teacher was invited to "be the sister cat today."

✔ **Extend children's play by modeling variations for children based on the content of their play.** As you do this take care not to depart from children's original ideas. Be alert to possible cues from children that your idea is not welcome. To extend upon Tanuka's interest in road building, one teacher put on a construction hat and walked into the block area with pad and pencil in hand to "inspect the work done so far." Tanuka's reaction was to say "Oops, bye!" and leave the area. The team members learned by observing Tanuka that they were more likely to be included in her play if they simply sat nearby and pushed the vehicles around in circles.

"The show is starting," Emma announces, as a way of inviting all who are interested to a music performance.

Indoor and Outdoor Materials to Add

Performances

1 If pretend performances have been a part of children's recent play, ask parents to save theater programs, movie ticket stubs, and boarding passes from special events they have experienced with their children. Add these materials to the block or house area.

2 To build on children's interest in performing, include a variety of recorded musical selections in the music area, for example, rock n' roll, opera, show music, country/western, blues recordings, and folk tunes such as those in the High/Scope Press *Rhythmically Moving* recording series.

Vehicles

3 To build on children's interest in construction vehicles, put props in the block area for pretend construction workers (hard hats, tool aprons).

4 Add an assortment of boxes to the house and block areas to provide enclosed spaces for animal homes or destinations for vehicle play. Cut out windows and doors in large appliance boxes and add these "buildings" to the outdoor environment. Leave them empty for several days; then fill them with little tables, sleeping bags, pillows, or soft cushions. If weather permits, keep some of the boxes outdoors on the playground and watch to see if they become destinations for riding toys.

A simple box added to the book area becomes a cozy "kitty basket" for Julia.

Prisons

5 If children have shown an interest in jails and law enforcement, add police officer props (pads for ticket writing, handcuffs, badges) to the block area.

6 Designate tiny spaces both indoors and outdoors to serve as pretend jails. The spaces should be enclosed but still visible. Equip each "jail" with a small cot, a chair, and some reading materials.

Animals

7 Put full cans and empty boxes of dog, cat, and bird food in the house area. Include leashes, collars, and food bowls with the stuffed animals.

8   Add storybooks about caring for pets and picture books about animals and their
    habitats to the book area, for example, *Puppy Love* by Madeline Sunshine, *If You
Give a Mouse a Cookie* by Laura Joffe Numeroff, and *The Little Rabbit* by Judy Dunn.

Planning and Recall Experiences

Performances

1   To build on the children's interest in performances,
    arrange chairs for your planning group in a semicircle.
Place a large hollow block in front of the chairs to make a
podium. Children can take turns standing on the hollow
block and performing in their own ways for the rest of the
group as they explain their plans or recall what they did
at work time. This strategy can be repeated over several
days by adding a new set of props each day. For example,
over four consecutive days you could introduce these
sets of props: (1) microphones and amplifiers, (2) musical
instruments, (3) tape recorders, and (4) programs for the
audience that list the order of turns for children's planning
and recalling. Some children will be interested in incorporating these props into their work time activities, so
continue to make them available at work time.

*Building on Caroline's interest in performances, this teacher
plays a cleanup game in which Caroline, using a pretend
microphone, tells her what to clean up next.*

Vehicles

2   To capitalize on children's interest in construction
    vehicles, take your planning/recall group and the dig-
ger truck to the sand table. To create individual containers
representing each of your classroom areas, make small
paper flags showing the symbols for each area, tape each
flag to a stick, and tape the sticks to individual plastic containers. Children can use the truck to dump a pile of sand
in the container that designates where they plan to work or
where they have worked. Realize that as a result of using
this planning/recall strategy, at work time some children
will probably choose to move materials from one area to
another. For example, they may play with the trucks at the sand table instead of
where you normally store them.

3   Bring small toy vehicles to the planning/recall table so each child has a vehicle
    in front of him or her. Set out area symbol cards and ask children to drive to
the area they plan to work in or to the place they enjoyed most during work time.
Determine whose turn is next by using an identical set of vehicles in a bag. Without

looking, the teacher or a child pulls a vehicle from the bag. The child whose vehicle matches the one pulled out of the bag is the next to plan or recall.

This child uses art materials to express her interest in vehicles.

4 This strategy is designed as a follow-up to strategy 3, "Small-Group Experiences," page 41. Ask children to find a partner and give each pair of children one of the cardboard boxes painted outdoors at small-group time. Ask children to sit in the boxes and pretend they are driving to or from school on a school bus. Encourage children to have a conversation with their partner about what they plan to do or what they did during work time. As work time starts, help children resolve conflicts, if they occur, about where to continue to work in their boxes. Setting up two rows of chairs side by side may provide similar conversational opportunities on another day. This seating arrangement can also be used if children are planning or recalling with the small group rather than in pairs. In this case, you might provide an old steering wheel found in an auto body shop or scrap yard as a prop for the child who is describing plans or experiences to the rest of the group. To vary this strategy on a different day, bring small toy school buses and small toy people to the planning/recall table. Using the toy figures as props, children can tell the school bus driver where to drop them off, depending on where they plan to work or where they have been during work time. One extension of this strategy is to use area symbol cards to designate certain areas of the planning table as the interest areas. As the bus driver stops at each card, the children who plan to work in that area or who worked in that area share their ideas.

Prisons

5 If prison-related play has been popular in your classroom, hold planning in a small enclosed space to capture the feeling of a jail cell. Lay out area symbol cards and tell children to pretend they are locked in a jail cell. Ask them to choose the card for the area they would play in if they had a key and could get out. As each child finishes planning, bring out a big cardboard key, pretend to unlock the "cell door," and let the child leave for work time.

Animals

6 To build on children's horse-related play, gather children indoors around a real horse saddle attached to a sawed-off tree stump or other sturdy structure. The person on the "horse" describes his or her plan and then gallops to that area. You can vary this strategy according to the type of animal play you have observed. For

example, you could have children plan or recall while curling up like cats in baskets or sitting inside cardboard doghouses or birdhouses.

7 Using animal puppets on one day and plastic animals on another, ask each child to pick an animal to be and to describe work time ideas to the rest of the "animal" group.

Small-Group Experiences

Performances

1 If you have observed pretend performances in your classroom, arrange a field trip to a local theater or auditorium where children are free to explore the stage and the seating arrangements. If possible, stay long enough either to watch a rehearsal or to interact with the performers while they are in costume or as they are applying their makeup.

2 Set up chairs to simulate auditorium or movie-theater seating. Give each child a ticket stub as he selects a place to sit. Read a short story such as Dr. Seuss's *The Cat in the Hat* "on stage" while children eat a snack of popcorn and juice. Then ask children to act out the parts of the story they remember. For example, if children remember the part where the cat comes in with the cleanup machine, they can move around the room making machine-like sounds and pretending to pick up toys with the machine.

Don't be surprised if a planning activity is so much fun for children that they continue it into work time. While teachers originally got out these puppets for children to use as planning props, these children have decided that playing with the puppets is their work time plan.

Vehicles

3 If vehicle play interests children in your group, try this strategy. Collect cardboard boxes large enough for children to sit in. Once you have collected one box for each child in your group, meet outside or in an open area of the classroom. Bring a variety of different-sized housepaint brushes and yellow, black, and red tempera paints. Let children paint the insides and outsides of the boxes. After the boxes dry, you can use them as "vehicles" at planning and recall times.

4 Call the city road department for information on local construction sites. Plan a field trip to watch large construction machinery in action. Help children focus on the sounds and smells produced by the various pieces of equipment. When you return to your center, give children markers, crayons, and paper and watch to see if they attempt to draw any aspect of their experience.

The availability of a collection of small vehicles enables this child to re-enact her experience with a real cherry-picker truck and to represent her understanding of how the truck worked.

5 Ask a local nursery to donate a pile of topsoil or sand to the school. Put a variety of large dump trucks, digger trucks, shovels, wagons, and buckets near the pile and watch as children move dirt or sand from one place to another. Use the dirt later for planting seeds and creating a space for a spring gardening project.

6 Put several small vehicles (diggers, dump trucks, garbage trucks, school buses, concrete mixers, cranes) in individual baskets for each child. Select vehicles that have moving parts children can manipulate. Provide loose materials collected from outside (for example, small twigs, leaves, wadded-up pieces of paper, chestnuts, and acorns) for children to use with the vehicles.

7 Suggest that children print with a variety of small toy vehicles and tempera paint. Children can dip the vehicles' wheels in paint and roll them across paper. Encourage children to notice the different kinds of imprints made by the various vehicles.

Prisons

8 Engage children in creative storytelling that builds on their interest in prisons and jails. Begin with an open-ended sentence, letting children fill in the rest of the story with their own words. As the story develops, keep the experience active by making motions and sound effects that connect to children's language. For example, you might start a story by saying "Today on the drive to school I saw a police car with the siren on [make a siren sound] and the lights flashing [make flashing motions with your hands by opening and closing them quickly]. When I looked more closely I saw my friend Greta in the car. She said to the police-woman: '_____' [let children finish]. Be creative in illustrating children's ideas with your motions and sound effects. If a child says, "Sorry, my car tire went flat," make a hissing sound to suggest air escaping from a tire. If children are new to creative storytelling, you may need to prompt them between ideas by repeating what they said and adding another sentence for them to complete. For example, to the child who talked about a flat tire, you might say, "'Your tire went flat' said the policewoman. 'Well, we'll have to call a _____.'"

Animals

9 If children in your group have been enjoying animal-related play, give each child an assortment of small toy animals and other materials for creative building and storytelling. Possible additional items (intended to be used on a succession of days, not all at once) include Play-Doh, inch-cube blocks, dominoes, yarn, string, pipe cleaners, blocks, paper clips, and shaving cream.

10 Read *Where the Wild Things Are* by Maurice Sendak. Afterward, ask children to re-enact the "wild rumpus." Hold the activity in a space that gives children

plenty of room for movement and provide a musical selection that encourages large and loud movements (for example, "Irish Washerwoman" from Volume 3 of High/Scope's *Rhythmically Moving* recording series). For added fun, take the group to a wooded area to replicate the forest in the book.

11 Give each child a crown-like piece of paper to decorate (similar to the hat Max wears in Sendak's *Where the Wild Things Are*) or a paper-towel tube to hold (like his scepter). Provide decorating materials, such as markers, crayons, watercolors, stickers, stamp pads and stampers, and glue with glitter and confetti. Children can save their creations for the next "wild rumpus" dance.

Large-Group Experiences

Performances

1 After you have observed pretend performances in the classroom, set up large blocks in a circle for children and adults to stand on. While standing on the blocks, the group can sing familiar songs, varying the way the songs are sung. For example, you may sing "Baa, Baa, Black Sheep" in a high voice, then "Twinkle, Twinkle, Little Star" in a low voice. You can also have children experiment with different volumes—singing softly or loudly, whispering, or soundlessly mouthing the words.

After a field trip to see the local high school band practice, this preschool class "plays instruments."

Vehicles

2 Vary the song "The Wheels on the Bus" by incorporating the various vehicles children play with or see on field trips. The new song might sound like this:

> The back of the dump truck goes up and down,
> Up and down, up and down.
> The back of the dump truck goes up and down.
> All through the town.

Additional verse ideas can come from the children.

Prisons

3 Provide another outlet for children's interest in prisons and police officers by singing or chanting the following song:

> Police officer, police officer,
> How very tall you are [stand tall],
> If all the cars will stop for you,
> As you hold out your hand [hold hand outstretched].

After singing, elicit children's ideas about what happens when the cars don't stop. Include their ideas in the next verse. Examples:

> Police officer, police officer,
> How very mad you'll get,
> If cars keep right on driving,
> When you hold out your hand.

> Police officer, police officer,
> The drivers go to jail,
> If cars keep right on driving,
> When you hold out your hand.

Animals

4 Sing and do the motions for the song "Horses Galloping." If possible designate a defined space, such as the perimeter of a large carpet, and gallop around it. Repeat the four lines to the chant over and over:

> Horses galloping, galloping, galloping,
> Clippety, clippety, clop,
> Horses galloping, galloping, galloping,
> Until the red light says stop.

Children can vary the "Horses Galloping" verse with other animal ideas. Examples: "Mice squeaking, squeaking," "Pigs oinking, oinking."

5 Play a freeze-action game with animal characters. Ask children to suggest an animal everyone can be and the action that animal makes. Some ideas might include galloping or neighing like a horse; meowing, scratching, or stretching like a kitty;

At Audie's suggestion, the group chants, "Mice squeaking, mice squeaking, mice squeaking..." as they move around the circle during large-group time. After this they try Megan's suggestion, "Kitties scratching."

barking like a dog; leaping like a frog; crawling like a snail; slithering like a snake; waddling like a duck; or flying like a bird. Put on music (for example, "Salty Dog Rag," Volume 9, *Rhythmically Moving*) and have children imitate the motion and the sound of the animal until the music stops and everyone freezes.

6 Set out the crown hats or toilet-paper tubes children decorated at small-group· time, play a music tape, and let children dance while balancing their hats on their heads. To vary the activity and add a conversation-starter, change the speed of the music so children can compare the ease of balancing their crowns during fast and slow movements.

What We Learned From Our Observations of Children

In this section we've presented a wide range of teaching strategies designed to support children's interest in creating pretend-play scenarios about performances, vehicles, prisons, and animals. On the next two pages we show some of the child anecdotes teachers recorded on the learning experiences that resulted when these teaching strategies were tried. The teachers classified these observations according to the High/Scope key experience categories.

Child Observations

CREATIVE REPRESENTATION

At planning time Alex pushed the digger truck back and forth through the dirt instead of pouring dirt into one of the area symbol containers.

As they were sitting in cardboard boxes at planning time, Keesha told Howard, "The bus hit a bumpy patch in the road." She began to bounce her body up and down and asked Howard to do the same.

At small-group time James covered the small toy horses and dogs with shaving cream. He told the adult that the animals were "trapped in the blizzard."

LANGUAGE AND LITERACY

*At greeting circle Carly went to the book area and paged through **Where the Wild Things Are** from beginning to end. She said the words "bad Max" as she looked at some of the pages near the front of the book and the words "still hot" as she got close to the end.*

At large-group time, when singing "The Wheels on the Bus," Sue suggested the verse "The hook on the tow truck picks up the car."

During a creative storytelling session at small-group time, Mark added these words to the story: "You can't arrest me. I have the power."

INITIATIVE AND SOCIAL RELATIONS

At planning time, before the others reached the table, Tanuka took her small toy car, drove it to the block area symbol, and said, "This is my plan. Bye." She then left the table and began working in the block area.

At work time when Jordan said, "No girls allowed by the trucks," Abby said, "My Daddy knows karate."

MOVEMENT

Abby pulled the wagon filled with dirt around the yard three times.

At large-group time James got down on the floor on his belly and wiggled across the rug to the suggestion "Slither like a snake."

While on the horse saddle at planning time, Mark moved in a back-and-forth motion, then tumbled off and said, "He bucked me."

MUSIC

Sue took a long wooden block to the music area, put on a tape, and pretended to strum the block to the beat of the music.

At large-group time Alex requested slower music because "The fast song makes my arms tired."

CLASSIFICATION

At planning time Tanuka pulled a toy school bus out of the bag and said, "Now it's Micah's turn." (Micah had the other school bus.)

At work time, while painting at the easel, Alex said, "Look, I used the brush to make long lines and to dab."

At outside time James said, "Snakes do not fly. Birds do."

SERIATION

At outside time Caitlin told Kyle, after filling a wagon with dirt, "Let's do another one that's not so big."

At large-group time, when playing "wild rumpus," Mark said, "I was fast, but this time I'll go faster."

While playing near the music area at work time, Abby shouted to some children who were playing tapes, "That's too loud. It hurts my ears, so make it softer."

NUMBER

When in the "planning jail," Colleen said, "Let's open the door after four people plan." After the fourth person planned she said, "Now it's time."

Keesha put two twigs in each of the small vehicles at work time, then said she was driving them "to the dump."

At planning time Brian said, "There're not enough chairs for all the children," then went to the computer area and brought back two more chairs.

SPACE

At small-group time Mark took the pipe cleaners, shaped them into rings, and placed them around the necks of the toy dogs.

At recall time, when asked to meow the next song, Tanuka asked if she could "meow it under the table."

When decorating her "Wild Things" crown at small-group time, Abby said, "I'm going to put blue next to red and then glitter in the middle."

TIME

While playing with the movie ticket stubs at work time, Julia told two other children, "I saw this a long, long, long, long, long, long time ago when Donald was just a little baby."

At small-group time Alex lined inch-cube blocks up in a circle, put a toy animal on top of each one, and said, "Now it's large-group time."

At planning time Sue said, "Yesterday we saw the big machines, and today I'm going to wear the hard hats."

Adult Training Activities

This training activity gives teachers practice in developing support strategies keyed to the specific interests children express as they pretend.

1. Ask workshop participants to read the following scenarios:

   At work time you observe James and Nanette dressing up in fancy clothes at the house area. James then brings a chair over to the sink and Nanette sits on it with her back to the sink. She leans her head back and James pretends to wash her hair. They then switch places and Nanette pretends to wash James's hair. Next they go to the art area, choose the thin colored pencils, and begin drawing on each other's faces. Next they use the magic markers to color each of the finger-nails on their hands. Finally they walk to an adult and say, "Will you marry us?"

   At outside time you see Erica pushing around a large Tinkertoy structure she made as she circles the grassy area of the playground. You make one just like hers and join her play by imitating her actions. She then says to you, "I already cut that part. You can cut over there." Meanwhile, Erin has put two round Tinkertoy pieces on each end of a long stick and is lifting them up and down over and over again. She hands the object to Cecelia and says, "Here, to make you strong."

   One of the children is about to return from a three-week holiday with his family in which he traveled by train to California to visit relatives. While there, the family visited Disneyland and stayed overnight at a hotel with a swimming pool and a hot tub.

2. Ask participants to develop several support strategies relating to one or more of the above play incidents for each of the categories below. The first strategy given in each category is an example to help participants get started.

General Teaching and Interaction Strategies

a. After you finish cutting where Erica tells you to, pause and wait for her reaction. For example, if she says, "Thanks. Now cut over here," move your "lawn mower" to the designated spot.

b.

Indoor and Outdoor Materials to Add

a. Add rakes, hoes, and shovels to the outdoor area.

b.

Planning and Recall Experiences

a. Bring to planning or recall time materials that capitalize on children's interest in hair washing. The person wearing a cape gets to plan or recall to the person holding the comb.

b.

Small-Group Experiences

a. Provide a variety of put-together-take-apart toys or materials (toothpicks with marshmallows or small table Tinkertoys, for example).

b.

Large-Group Experiences

a. Sing the following song, with motions:

>   **Verse One:**
>   The train is a comin', oh yeah,
>   The train is a comin', oh yeah,
>   The train is a comin',
>   The train is a comin',
>   The train is a comin', oh yeah,

Repeat the sequence with the following verses:

>   **Verse Two:** Come and get your ticket right here.
>   **Verse Three:** Goin' up the mountain so slow.
>   **Verse Four:** Comin' down the mountain so fast.
>   **Verse Five:** Pull into the station, slow down.

b.

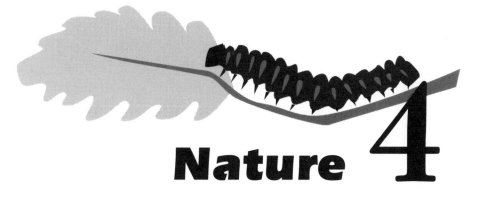

Nature 4

Observing Plants,

Animals, and

Weather

At outside time Kayla suddenly stops her bicycle in the middle of a sidewalk. *She gets off the bike and lies on the ground on her side. Her eyes follow the movements of a single ant across the concrete. Later during that same outside time, Kayla calls a teacher over to ask about a caterpillar she has noticed on the underside of a tree leaf. The next day Kayla notices that the same leaf has broken off the tree and that the caterpillar is still on the leaf but looks different. Kayla brings the caterpillar and the leaf to her teacher, who explains that the caterpillar has dried out because it needed the leaf as a food source to grow into a butterfly. Kayla then asks, "Can I go inside to get some tape so I can tape the leaf back on the tree?"*

Kacey calls across the play yard to Julia, Emma, and Jordan, who are swinging on a tire swing: "You just won't believe it! Come here, come here!" Only Julia comes to join Kacey. Together the girls bend over to examine the ground closely. "Flowers, flowers poking out. Tiny, purple ones. Yeah! Yeah! Yeah!" Kacey chants as they jump up and down together.

On Monday morning Mrs. Abelson, Donald's mom, reports that she and her family visited her sister over the weekend. She explains that her sister lives near a wooded area with a pond and that the family collected some tadpoles there that she and Donald want to add to the preschool. She describes how, during a walk through the woods, Donald noticed various animal tracks, and stopped several times to say, "Mommy, what made this mark?" As his mother talks to the teacher, Donald carries the container of tadpoles to the greeting circle and puts it on the floor. When Leah presses her nose against the container, Donald says, "Look, they're swimming all around inside there." As greeting time ends, the teacher asks Donald to suggest a safe place to store the tadpoles. He replies, "On top of the cubbies."

⟳

Alex is digging for worms at outside time. Holding a worm in his hand, he walks over to an adult and says, "Look what I found." To acknowledge his effort the teacher says, "You found a worm that wiggles." "I did, and I'm going back to dig again with the shovel to see if I can find ten more," Alex replies. He begins digging again, carefully lining up each new worm he finds next to the others on the sidewalk.

⟳

Moments before outside time is scheduled to begin, a thunderstorm rolls into the area. As if the lights had been switched off, the classroom suddenly darkens. Thunder booms, lightning flashes, and sheets of rain pour from the sky, hitting the sliding glass doors. Several children gather at the book area, which is the usual meeting place when outside time has to be canceled. Others cluster around one of the teachers, Philip, who is standing near the window watching the storm. Some children stay at the small-group time tables and continue to work with the materials available that day.

In the house area, Erica picks up the play phone, dials a few numbers, and says, "Brett, you better come get me." After waiting at the door for a few minutes, she comes back, dials again, and says, "Nine-one-one! Come get me, there's a storm coming." Finally she takes a baby doll, sits down with it on the pillows in the book area, and cries softly. A few minutes later 3-year-old Glen puts his arm around Erica and says, "Don't worry. The angels are having a picnic, and they're rolling the barrels of birch beer."

By positioning yourself at children's physical level you let them know you share their interests and are available to interact with them as they explore nature.

Supporting Children's Learning Outdoors: The Adult Role

Young children are curious about the natural world. As they observe the world around them, they notice many similarities and differences;

they are fascinated with the ways their outside environment changes over time. Watching young children explore their outdoor environment is a special treat for adults, who often gain a better understanding of the interests and ability levels of individual children. They may notice, for example, that a child who typically plays one way in the indoor environment breaks out of this pattern when in an outdoor environment. Cecelia, for example, usually played by herself indoors and rarely played without her favorite blanket nearby. When outside, however, Cecelia sometimes became boisterous and social. One day at outside time Cecelia surprised her teacher by playfully barricading the stairs to the top of the tree house. As the teacher tried to climb the stairs, Cecelia stretched out her legs to bar the way, pointing a finger at the teacher and saying "You can't come up here because I have the power." A contrasting example is Audie. Inside the classroom Audie would often make plans that involved lots of physical activity with other children. He especially enjoyed enlisting his peers in jumping off staircases or pieces of furniture or in moving around the bookcases, couch, and chairs in the book area. Outdoors, however, Audie's play sometimes was much more quiet and solitary. One day at outside time, an adult observed Audie lying flat on his back and looking up at the sky. The adult quietly lay down near him and overheard him saying "Those clouds look like cotton candy, but they're moving slowly."

When adults strive to match children's enthusiasm and curiosity about the world around them, children learn that their interests are valued and important.

Some adults do not join readily in the wider range of play experiences that occur in an outdoor space; they may feel uncomfortable with the idea of lying down on a grassy hill next to a child. In the High/Scope approach, however, we view the role of adults at outside time as similar to their role at work time; at both times we encourage adults to be actively involved in children's play. While adults may be tempted to use outside time as their break time, we ask instead that they keep their attention focused on understanding and supporting children's interests and play ideas. When adults help children explore and experience the outdoor world—including natural materials such as leaves, rocks, shells, sticks, and dirt as well as the changing conditions created by wind, fog, rain, sunshine, and snow—they are helping children develop an appreciation of nature. Adults are also supporting a wide range of cognitive, physical, and social learning experiences.

The anecdotes that open this chapter are typical of these outdoor learning experiences. To document the learning that occurred in these incidents, teachers recorded the anecdotes that appear on the next page. As they discussed these incidents, teachers used the High/Scope Child Observation Record (COR) as a framework for understanding the developmental significance of their observations. Next to each anecdotal note is the COR item the teachers matched it with.

Supporting Children's Curiosity About Nature

What children learn from their outdoor activities is influenced by the actions and attitudes of their primary caregivers. Consider the anecdote about Alex, who proudly showed a worm to his teacher. If the teacher had responded, "Ooh, Alex, that worm's dirty and has germs. Please put it back on the ground and go inside and wash your hands," Alex's curiosity would have been stifled. Likewise, Kayla's curiosity about the ant might have been dampened if an adult had told her, "Lying on the sidewalk in the middle of a bike path is dangerous. You should get up!"

The day after children noticed caterpillars outside, the teacher reads the story The Very Hungry Caterpillar.

An adult's timing in responding to children's explorations also has an impact on children's learning. There are moments when it is important for the adult to hold back; the adult may interrupt or interfere with the child's learning process by getting involved too quickly in the child's activity. During the thunderstorm incident, when Erica telephoned for help, the teacher's first impulse was to run to Erica and comfort her. However, this would have robbed Erica and Glen of the opportunity to handle the situation on their own, in a way that made sense to them. At other times, it's appropriate for teachers to respond quickly to children's new-found interests by providing additional materials and experiences that will expand and broaden the children's learning.

The teachers did this when they supported Donald's new interest in tadpoles by immediately making room for them in the classroom. By responding in this way, the teachers helped Donald tie his home activities into school life and provided an experience with long-term learning value.

Following are strategies for supporting children as they explore nature, presented in terms of the play examples that open this chapter and the specific interests children expressed in plants, ants, and caterpillars; tadpoles and ponds; dirt and worms; and thunderstorms.

Child Observations

INITIATIVE

Teacher's Anecdotal Notes	*High/Scope COR Item and Level*
After showing Beth the worm at outside time, Alex said, "I'm going back to dig again with the shovel and see if I can find ten more."	A. Expressing choices: (4) Child indicates with a short sentence how plans will be carried out.
At outside time Kayla noticed a dried caterpillar hanging from a broken leaf. She asked Carol [the teacher], "Can I go inside to get some tape so I can tape the leaf back on the tree?"	B. Solving problems: (3) Child uses one method to try to solve a problem, but if unsuccessful, gives up after one or two tries.
At outside time Kayla rode the bicycle down part of the sidewalk, then got off and watched a tiny ant crawl across the asphalt.	C. Engaging in complex play: (2) Child shows interest in simple use of materials or simple participation in activities.
At small-group time as a thunderstorm approached, Erica went to the house area, picked up the phone, dialed several numbers, and said into the phone,"Brett, you better come get me." Then she went to the door and stood for a minute, after which she came back, picked up the phone, and said, "Nine-one-one, come get me, there's a storm coming." Last, she took a baby doll from the house area to the book area, sat down with the doll, began crying softly, and said, "I want the thunder to stop now."	C. Engaging in complex play: (3) Child, acting alone, uses materials or organizes active play involving two or more steps.

SOCIAL RELATIONS

Teacher's Anecdotal Notes	*High/Scope COR Item and Level*
At outside time Alex ran to Beth [the teacher] with a worm in his hand and said, "Look what I found."	E. Relating to adults: (3) Child initiates interactions with familiar adults.
At small-group time, after Glen put his arm around her and told her not to worry about the thunderstorm, Erica moved her body closer to his.	F. Relating to other children: (2) Child responds when other children initiate interactions.

LOGIC AND MATHEMATICS

Teacher's Anecdotal Notes	*High/Scope COR Item and Level*
At greeting time, when asked where a safe place to store the tadpoles would be, Donald said, "On top of the cubbies."	CC. Describing spatial relations: (3) Child uses words that describe the relative positions of things.
At outside time Kacey jumped up and down and chanted, "Flowers, flowers, poking out."	CC. Describing spatial relations: (4) Child uses words that describe the direction of movement of things.

The teacher's role in the outdoor environment is the same as it is indoors—to observe and support children's interests by following the children's cues.

General Teaching and Interaction Strategies

✔ **Let children experiment and follow through on their ideas, even when you know they won't work.** When Kayla asked if she could tape the leaf with the caterpillar back on the tree, the teachers knew that it would not bring the caterpillar back to life. Still, they encouraged her to try out her idea. When the caterpillar still hung limply the next day, Kayla had an opportunity to talk about her observations as well as her feelings of disappointment and sadness.

✔ **Remember that sometimes your best interaction strategy is simply to watch and record what children do and how they react.** During the thunderstorm, for example, the teachers learned a lot about Erica and Glen from their different reactions. During work time Erica often became involved in role-play situations, so it made sense to the adults that she would rely on her imagination to help her work through her discomfort with the storm. When she began crying quietly, the teacher's decision to stand back for a moment gave Glen the chance to be the person who supported her. Observing Glen gave the teachers valuable information about his ability to consider the feelings of others.

✔ **Give children the chance to describe, in their own words, the experiences that are meaningful to them.** After Donald brought in the tadpoles, the teachers

Let children know their ideas and interests are welcomed in the classroom by encouraging them to describe, in their own words, their outside-of-class experiences (like catching these tadpoles).

referred children to Donald when they asked what the tadpoles were or where they came from. When children asked additional questions like "What's a pond?" the teachers again called upon Donald's expertise: "Donald, Megan would like to know what a pond is. Can you tell her what the pond that you visited was like?"

✔ **Show support for children's interests by matching their enthusiasm.** When Julia and Kacey discovered the blooming crocus plants, a teacher matched their excitement by jumping up and down with them. Similarly, when Alex discovered the worm and brought it to the teacher, vowing to go back and dig for ten more worms, the teacher wondered to herself how she could support Alex's new plan. A while later, observing that he was digging again and had laid several more worms out on the sidewalk, she decided to help him reach his goal. She went over to the spot where he had been digging, knelt down on the ground, and began digging alongside him. They continued digging together and laying worms side by side until Alex announced that they had enough worms.

Indoor and Outdoor Materials to Add

Plants, ants, and caterpillars

1 To build on children's interest in flowers and how they grow, visit a local farmers market or nursery in the fall and let each child pick out several spring bulbs. Provide a variety of diggers (trowels, spades, shovels, and spoons) and have children plant some of their bulbs in individual containers and others in the ground. In the

spring observe and record children's reactions as the plants grow and bloom. Give children their potted plants to take home.

2   Cut some branches and place them in a plastic container of water so children may observe the buds opening up. Horse chestnut, forsythia, and magnolia branches are best to try. To give children an opportunity to experience the smells of different plants, add lilac branches to the classroom when they are in bloom.

3   Plant fast-growing items like grass seed, lima beans, or alfalfa sprouts with children, both indoors and outdoors. (Alfalfa seeds will produce edible sprouts if rinsed daily and kept moist in a jar.)

4   Dig gullies in the dirt near places where you see ants crawling and fill them with tiny crumbs of food to attract the ants. Watch with the children as ants gather and move food particles from one area to another.

5   Add the book *The Very Hungry Caterpillar* by Eric Carle to your book area. Make the story come alive for the children by drawing pictures of food items like those in the story, cutting them out, and laminating them. Make the pictures large enough so there is room for a hole in the middle of each one the size of a child's wrist. (This loosely simulates the appearance of the book, which has holes in the pages big enough to poke a finger through.) To represent the caterpillar, provide socks for children to fit over their hands and forearms. Encourage children to use the food pictures as props as they participate in telling the story, slipping pictures of food items over their sock-covered hands as the caterpillar in the story eats the various foods.

Tadpoles and ponds

6   If children, like Donald, are excited about a recent experience with tadpoles or other pond creatures, put a container of tadpoles in the classroom at the children's eye level. Add magnifying glasses so children can more easily see the tadpoles' movements as they swim through the water.

7   Bring the pond materials children collected at small-group time (see strategy 4, "Small-Group Experiences," page 61) back to school and add them to the interest areas suggested by children.

Dirt and worms

8   To capitalize on children's interest in observing worms, make two worm farms by filling clear plastic containers with alternating 1-inch layers of soil and sand. Put a few worms in each container, then cover the top with a layer of dead leaves. Leave one container open and set it out for children to watch; cover the other with a dark cloth and tell children you are putting it away for five days. To help children anticipate when the cover will be removed from this container, you could blow up five balloons and pop one each day, uncovering the container when there are no balloons left. Encourage children to notice and compare the changes that have occurred in the two containers as a result of the worms' work.

9 With the help of your parent group, build a small compost pile. Since children enjoy sorting, encourage children to sort the plates, utensils, food scraps, and waste paper after snacks or mealtimes. With the children, choose some categories for sorting, for example, "Things for the garbage can," "Things to put in the dishwasher," "Things to be recycled," and "Things to toss into the compost pile." Encourage children to look for the worms that eat the compost.

10 With the help of interested children, haul the sand out of the sand table and replace it with soil, dirt, or gravel. Add shovels, spoons, and a container of plastic worms. Watch as children have fun burying, burrowing for, and finding the worms.

Thunderstorms

11 The day after a thunderstorm, put a variety of spray bottles at the water table and add hoses, nozzles, and sprinklers to the outdoor area so children can pretend to make their own rainstorms.

12 Put raincoats, boots, rain bonnets and hats, and umbrellas in the dress-up area.

13 Include flashlights, drums, and other noise-making instruments in the music area so children can make their own pretend thunder and lightning.

14 Add books like *Rain,* by Peter Spier, and *Rain Makes Applesauce,* by Julian Scheer, to the book area so children can read stories about, and enjoy photos of, rain and thunderstorms.

Planning and Recall Experiences

Plants, ants, and caterpillars

1 While it is important to prepare in advance for each day's planning and recall times, it is also important to be spontaneous and ready to change your plans at a moment's notice.

The sound-making materials teachers added to the classroom help children re-create the sounds of a recent thunderstorm.

One teacher's most memorable planning time occurred when a bug happened to crawl up the table leg as planning time was about to begin. Instead of trying to distract the children, who were avidly watching the bug, the teacher simply said, "Whichever child the bug crawls closest to will be the first one to share plans with the rest of us." For as long as the bug cooperated, the group continued to let it decide whose turn it was to plan.

2 To follow up on children's enthusiasm about ants and caterpillars, tie a string to a plastic ant or caterpillar and ask children to move it from one person to another. The person holding the creature is the next to share work time plans or experiences.

3 To build on the children's interest in things that grow outdoors, bring several identical boxes with lids to your group. Put a bunch of dandelions in one box, and keep the other boxes empty. Play a musical selection, (such as "Spring" from Vivaldi's *Four Seasons*) and have children pass the boxes around the group in musical-chairs fashion. When the music stops, ask the children to look inside the boxes. The child whose box has the dandelion bunch is the next to describe work time plans or experiences.

4 Make cards shaped like the outdoor creatures children are interested in (for example, spider, ant, butterfly, caterpillar, and bumblebee) and write the symbols for the interest areas on the cards. Laminate the cards and put paper clips on each one. Have children use a magnet attached to a string to "fish" for the card representing the area they plan to play in (or have played in) and describe their ideas.

5 With the children, crawl "like an ant" or "like a caterpillar" to the various interest areas. When the group reaches each interest area, the children who plan to work there (or who worked there that day) share their ideas.

Tadpoles and ponds

6 If children have shown an interest in animal footprints, try this strategy: Have children sit on the floor so they can see the bottoms of one another's shoes. While the others close their eyes, ask two children at a time to make a footprint in a slab of Play-Doh. Let the other children guess whose foot made each print, and then ask the child who made the footprint to plan or recall.

7 Spread out interest area symbol cards over a large section of the floor. Put on a musical recording (for example, "The Hustle" from Volume 9 of the High/Scope Press *Rhythmically Moving* series) and while it is playing, ask children to swim like tadpoles. When the music stops ask children to "swim to" a symbol card for their chosen interest area and talk about their plans or experiences.

Dirt and worms

8 If digging for worms has been a popular activity during outside time, fill the sand and water table with dirt and plastic worms as described in strategy 10, "Indoor and Outdoor Materials to Add," page 59. Ask children to take turns finding a hidden worm. When a child finds a worm, it is his or her turn to talk about work time plans or experiences.

9 Vary strategy 3 by putting a real or construction-paper worm in one of the boxes instead of the dandelions.

Thunderstorms

10 Use thunderstorm-related props (for example, an umbrella, hat, or raincoat) for planning or recalling. Pass the prop for the day to the child whose turn is next. The child wears the item while describing his or her plans or experiences.

11 Give the child who is planning or recalling a flashlight. Ask the child to "shine the flashlight like a lightning flash" in the area where he or she plans to be (or has been) during work time.

Small-Group Experiences

Plants, ants, and caterpillars

1 Provide trowels, shovels, spoons, plastic containers, and grass seed. Watch which children use the materials to fill and empty and which children plant and then care for the grass seed.

2 Read the book *The Very Hungry Caterpillar* to the children. Then give each child a paper tube containing a rolled-up piece of paper. Also set out markers, crayons, glue, and glitter and suggest that children use the materials to make a butterfly.

3 Provide a collection of natural items—tree branches, long grasses, leaves—and colored yarn and tape. Encourage children to try various ways of attaching the items to the tree branches.

Tadpoles and ponds

4 If some children in your classroom, like Donald, have talked about their pond experiences, introduce other children to ponds or pond creatures by taking a walk near a pond. Encourage children to collect stones, sticks, bird feathers, plants, and whatever else they can find. Talk with them about where they would like to store the items when they return to school.

5 Purchase or make ink stamps in the shapes of tadpoles or other natural creatures and materials you saw on your pond trip (ducks, toads, birds, sticks, plants). (You can make simple stamps by cutting sponges or pieces of soft plastic foam into various shapes and gluing them to small blocks of wood.) Provide paper, ink pads, and markers to use with the stamps and suggest that children create their own pond stories.

6 Save some of the materials collected on the pond walk and set them out with trays of paint and paper. Encourage children to print with the objects by dipping them in the paint and stamping them on the paper.

7 Take a field trip to a local pet store where children can see a variety of fish swimming in tanks.

Dirt and worms

8 If children have shown an interest in worms, pass out chocolate sandwich cookies and encourage children to mash and crumble them into a bowl. Add Gummy Bear worms and have the children pretend they are eating dirt and worms.

9 Provide individual trays of dirt for each child to explore. Include some of the following materials to use with the dirt: real or plastic worms, magnifying lens, small vehicles (tractor, bulldozer, dump truck), tongue depressors.

10 Purchase a quantity of plastic worms, lizards, or other similar "critters" in the fishing department of a discount store. Provide each child with a few worms of different colors and a clear plastic cup (the worms will stick to the cup). You may also add water as a back-up material.

Thunderstorms

11 To capture the excitement generated by a thunderstorm, provide materials children can use in re-enacting it. Materials could include scarves to make the wind, flashlights to make lightning, drums to make thunder, and rice in a shaker to simulate rainfall. After children select their materials, put on music (for example, Tchaikovsky's *1812 Overture*) and observe their actions and sounds.

12 Hold small-group time outside on a day when there is a light, misty rain. Provide dry tempera paints inside shaker bottles. As children sprinkle paint on colored paper, watch and record their reactions as they observe what happens when the raindrops fall on the powdered paints.

13 Read a story about rain and give children one of the props listed in strategy 11 for making "special effects." (Use a variety of props rather than all one kind.) Select a key word repeated often in the story (*storm, rain, thunder, lightning*) and ask children to use their props to make their special effects each time they hear the word. (Don't expect preschool children to match the visual or sound effects with the corresponding word. Just pick one word and have children use all the props together each time the word is spoken.)

Large-Group Experiences

Plants, ants, and caterpillars

1 Build on the children's experience with creatures in their world by singing a variation of the song "The Green Grass Grew All Around" that relates the child's experiences. Incorporate the children's additional ideas. The following version is built

When you provide new experiences, watch for the things that interest children, then plan follow-up experiences. Following this field trip, teachers planned a large-group time in which children recalled the movements and sounds of the wild geese.

on Kayla's experience with the caterpillar:

> There was a caterpillar in the middle of the leaf,
> The prettiest leaf that you ever did see,
> And the cocoon it grew all around, all around,
> And the cocoon it grew all around.

> Now in that cocoon, there was a butterfly,
> The prettiest butterfly that you ever did see,
> And the cocoon it grew all around, all around,
> And the cocoon it grew all around.

2   Ask children for their ideas on how an ant would crawl if it had a huge, heavy piece of bread in its mouth or how it would feel to be a crocus poking its head out of the ground. Put on music that has two distinct parts (such as "La Raspa" from Volume 3, *Rhythmically Moving*) and have the children act out their ant-movement idea during one part and the flower idea during the second part.

Tadpoles and ponds

3   Change the words to the song "Down in the Meadow" so that it focuses on tadpoles and ponds:

> Down in the meadow in an itty bitty pond,
> Swam three little tadpoles, and a mama tadpole, too.
> "Swim," said the mama, "as fast as you can,"
> And they swam and they swam all over the pond.

Boom, boom, didum dadum, wadum, shoo.
[Repeat twice]
And they swam and they swam all over the pond.

4 Make tadpoles out of heavy oak tag paper, one for each child in the group. Spread the paper tadpoles over a large area of the floor. Play a musical selection (for example, "The Dance of the Sugar Plum Fairy" from Tchaikovsky's *Nutcracker*) and ask children to move around the paper tadpoles to the music. Whenever the music stops, each child finds a tadpole to stand on and a new child suggests the next way the group will move to the music, for example, crawling, walking backwards, making swimming movements.

Dirt and worms

5 Sing songs about dirt and worms to the tune of "Twinkle, Twinkle, Little Star," for example,

Earthworms, earthworms, in the ground,
Earthworms, earthworms, digging round.
Earthworms, earthworms, digging deep,
Earthworms, earthworms do they sleep?
[Repeat first two lines to complete song.]

Of, if a child, like Alex, has been digging for and counting worms, sing "One Little, Two Little, Three Little Earthworms" to the tune of the familiar song.

Thunderstorms

6 Take the whole group outside after a rainstorm or thunderstorm has subsided. (Wait until the thunder and lightning have stopped and the rain has slowed to a drizzle.) Gather in a place that is sheltered from the rain. Huddle close together. (On a foggy day, meet in the haze of the fog.) Go back to the same place on a bright sunny day and observe which children comment on the difference: then consider how this relates to children's developing classification and language skills.

What We Learned From Our Observations of Children

In this chapter we've presented a variety of teaching strategies for building on children's experiences with nature. When these strategies were tried, teachers recorded a wide range of child anecdotes on the resulting learning experiences. On pages 65–66 we present excerpts from these anecdotal notes, and show how teachers classified the notes according to the High/Scope key experience categories. As they interpreted their observations according to the High/Scope key experiences, teachers realized that children were using a variety of cognitive, social, and physical abilities as they explored nature.

Child Observations

CREATIVE REPRESENTATION

At small-group time Rebecca painted with a bird feather collected on the pond walk. She brushed the feather back and forth in the middle of her paper, using the feather as a paintbrush. Next she used the feather like a stamp, making prints of the feather all around the border of the paper.

Frances chose the bumblebee-shaped magnet at planning time, buzzing it over to Megan's foot and saying, "Ouch, it stung you."

LANGUAGE AND LITERACY

At small-group time, when sprinkling tempera paint on paper in the rain, Tylon said, "Look, it's crying."

At large-group time, Kayla suggested adding this verse to the caterpillar song:

> *Now, on one day, the butterfly cracked out.*
> *The prettiest butterfly that you ever did see.*
> *And the cocoon it fell on the ground, on the ground.*
> *And the cocoon it fell on the ground."*

INITIATIVE AND SOCIAL RELATIONS

At small-group time Monica was pressing the animal-shaped stamps on a piece of paper and some ink got on her fingers. She got out a paper towel and rubbed at the spot. When the spot didn't come off, she wet the paper towel and rubbed the spot again. When this didn't work, she went to the sink and lathered her hands with soap and water.

During small-group time, as children used various materials to make butterflies, James turned to Audie and said, "That's nice, because you're my best friend."

MOVEMENT

At work time Madison put on a raincoat, snapped four of the snaps, went over to the teacher, and said, "Look, I snapped them all by myself."

At large-group time Nathaniel made big, fluttering motions with his arms when Kayla described the butterfly "cracking out" of the cocoon.

MUSIC

During the pond walk, a blue jay sang. Jaleesa responded, "What's that noise?"

During large-group time, Emma stretched her whole body out on the floor and slithered across the movement area. When the music stopped, she jumped up, ran over to an oak tag tadpole, and jumped on it.

At small-group time, right before the start of outside time, Kacey began singing, "Rain, rain go away. Come again another day. I would like to go out and play."

Continued on the next page.

Continued from the previous page.

CLASSIFICATION

After returning from the pet store, Erica went to the tadpole container and said, "Hey, little tadpoles. You're much smaller than those big fish."

At recall time Madison said, "I wore the raincoat, but not the hat."

At small-group time Sue took the fish stampers and put them in the middle of her paper. Next she took a blue marker, drew an oval shape that enclosed all the fish, and said, "This is the pond where they swim."

SERIATION

During our rainy-day small-group time, Glen set down the powder-paint picture he had made and jumped up and down near it. He said, "Look, the rain makes my paint runnier."

At small-group time, after making his butterfly, James tossed it into the air and said to Audie and Sam, "Mine is the fastest flyer."

At small-group time Trey gathered three bird feathers he had collected on the pond walk and arranged them from largest to smallest on construction paper. He pointed to them one at a time, saying "Small, smaller, smallest."

NUMBER

At work time, Zoe took sticks and lined them up side by side in a row. When she was finished lining up ten sticks, she got the box of stones and put one stone at the top of each stick.

At small-group time Becky said to Tucker, "Pass me a lot of those grass seeds. I'm going to plant a bunch."

After a trip to the pet store, Jeremy told his Dad (who was picking him up), "We saw the most of the fish and only one snake."

SPACE

At small-group time, as Brendan tied yarn to a tree branch, he said, "It hangs all the way down here low."

At small-group time Jordan used a slotted spoon to scoop dirt back and forth between two plastic containers, filling one container, then emptying it to fill the other.

At work time, as Alice was burying plastic worms in the dirt, she repeated, "Under the ground, back up again."

TIME

When outside time ended, Alex said, "I couldn't find ten more worms. Maybe tomorrow."

At planning time Julia swam like a tadpole while the music played and went right to the block area symbol when the music stopped. She sat down and said, "I'm going to work here today."

When Erica gave her mom the flowering spring bulb she had planted in the fall, she said, "First we put it in the ground, then we put it away to sleep, now it's a pretty present for you."

Adult Training Activities

To help participants understand the amount of learning that can take place when they build on children's interest in nature, ask them to choose one of the following three settings in which to observe and record the actions of children. After they return from observing in the setting, have them classify their notes on children's actions according to the High/Scope key experiences or the High/Scope Child Observation Record (COR). Give participants the following directions:

Choose one of the three settings below for observing children:

- ***Setting One:*** *Visit a local neighborhood park.*

- ***Setting Two:*** *Visit a neighborhood swimming pool.*

- ***Setting Three:*** *Take children outdoors during the first snowfall of the year or on a particularly foggy day.*

If you have chosen Setting One or Two, choose a partner and quietly and unobtrusively observe the children at play for 30 minutes. Record the language, actions, and interactions of the children. Compare notes with your partner only after the observation is finished. Then work together to categorize your findings according to the High/Scope key experiences or the High/Scope Child Observation Record (COR) categories. If you have chosen Setting Three, enjoy your involvement with the children and make a conscious effort to use some of the recommended adult-child interaction strategies as you work with them. Discuss your findings at the end of the school day with your team member.

Social Play 5

Exploring

Feelings and

Relationships

Two weeks ago, 3-year-old Saraya's family role changed from "only child" to "big sister." Since then, Saraya's teachers have noticed that she often makes plans to play in the house area. Her play usually follows the same pattern: she removes all the baby dolls from the doll bed, throws them down next to her on the floor, climbs into the bed, and lies there, sucking her fingers and saying "Waaa, waaa, waaa" over and over. When she does this, one of the teachers often sits next to Saraya, patting her gently on the back and ignoring the dolls she has thrown on the floor.

As the weeks pass Saraya begins to spend less time in the doll bed crying and more time interacting with the doll babies, pretending to change their diapers or feed them in the high chair. As before, a teacher often joins Saraya by playing next to her. One day a teacher watches as Saraya places her doll in the high chair. Saraya holds the doll in place with one hand and stretches out the other to reach the neckties in the nearby dress-up clothes. She then uses the tie to strap her doll securely into the chair. On another day the adult watches as Saraya takes a diaper wrap, opens it flat on the table, and puts the baby doll on top of it. She then leaves for a moment to get a Kleenex, uses it to swab the baby's bottom, then fastens the Velcro closing on the diaper wrap. As Saraya works, she says, "Ooh, you stink." After pretending to swish the old diaper in the toy washing machine, she puts the doll back in the bed (where dolls are stored when not in use), and leaves the area to paint a picture at the easel.

In the middle of planning time, Ashley, who usually relates her plans verbally before beginning work time, leaves the table suddenly and without speaking. She goes to the house area, gets a flight bag, and packs it with doll and child clothing, carefully folding each item before she puts it in the bag. When she is finished packing the bag, she tosses it over her shoulder, picks up two dolls from the doll bed, and goes to the block area. She sits down on a block near some other children and asks, "When's the next plane to Florida?"

After a moment she says, "I'm getting off the plane." Then she gets up, taking her bag and babies, and walks over to the book area. There she sits down next to a teacher and says, "Kevin drank too much beer and said, '____ you!' so I took the kids away for two weeks." Her teacher waits a moment until she is sure Ashley is finished talking and says, "Oh. Kevin drank too much and used harsh language, so you decided to take the kids away for two weeks." Ashley nods and Alex, who has listened to the exchange, leans closer to Ashley, puts his hand on her shoulder and says, "There really wasn't anything else you could do."

At work time Audie and James are playing with the Old Maid card game in the house area. Audie shuffles and deals the cards and they begin taking turns picking cards from each other's hands and laying the matched pairs face up on the table. Erica walks up and asks if she can join the game. The boys say yes.

When Erica joins in, she plays without any sense of the conventional rules, taking more than one card at a time, holding her matched pairs in her hand, and saying "Oh, darn—I didn't get her" when she doesn't succeed in picking the Old Maid card. James and Audie respond by trying to explain the rules, saying things like: "No, hold your cards the other way so James can't see them." "Not now, your turn is after Audie's turn." "You're only supposed to take one card." "You mean, you don't have a match yet?" "You're supposed to try NOT to get the Old Maid!" After one round, Erica says, "Oh brother," and leaves the table. Audie and James giggle and continue to play without her.

Leah and Megan, who are pretending to be dogs, crawl into the block area where Daniel and Victor are building. The two girls face Daniel and Victor and make loud barking noises. Daniel says, "You need a dog house," and he and Victor begin reshaping their block structure so it encloses Leah and Megan. The girls continue to bark and howl. Soon Alex comes over and says, "Hey, let's have a dog show." He goes to the art area and returns with paper, scissors, markers, and tape for making "prize ribbons." While Alex is working, Daniel and one of the teachers join in making ribbons. As they work, the teacher says, "I wonder what kinds of prizes the dogs will be awarded." Daniel suggests that the prizes go to "the loudest" and "the one that sleeps the most." After the ribbons are completed, Alex asks the teacher to write Daniel's words on the ribbons.

Building Self-Awareness and Social Abilities Through Play

Preschoolers are aware of and interested in people and their relationships. You can see this interest in their play as they imitate the actions of their caregivers and playmates. You can also observe it as they notice the comings and goings of important people in their playmates' lives, for example as Audie shouts, "Leah, your nanny is coming," when he sees the nanny's car pulling into the parking lot.

The play examples that open this chapter all reflect preschoolers' growing social awareness.

Three friends tuck their dog into bed before leaving for the "party dance."

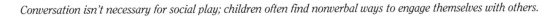

Conversation isn't necessary for social play; children often find nonverbal ways to engage themselves with others.

A problem leads to a cooperative solution as children join together to move the table.

Sometimes this interest in personal relationships and feelings is expressed very directly, as in the case of Saraya, who explores her feelings about the addition of a new family member through her pretend play with dolls. Similarly, Ashley uses pretending to express her concerns about a family conflict she has apparently witnessed.

Another way preschoolers express their interest in people and relationships is through their developing interest in collaborative activities, such as the Old Maid game that Erica, Audie, and James are playing. Preschoolers are just beginning to develop the thinking abilities needed to play conventional games with rules and turn-taking. As these new abilities emerge, the process of learning the rules (or developing their own ways to play) is a social experience that involves exchanging ideas and negotiation. Some children, like Erica, are not yet developmentally ready to play by the official rules, yet enjoy participating. Whether children follow conventional rules or develop their own rules, taking part in a game is an important social experience that strengthens their capacities for collaborating with others.

Another form of collaborative play is social pretending, in which children work together to develop complex play dramas. The dog show scenario of Leah, Megan, Daniel, and Victor is an example of this kind of cooperative effort, in which each child contributes ideas and builds on the ideas of others. Unlike Saraya and Ashley, these children are not directly depicting family life in their play. Yet their interest in caregiving and personal relationships is clearly expressed as they pretend to be dogs and dog-owners.

As preschoolers engage in social play experiences like these, they are developing social awareness, the ability to collaborate with others, and skills in many other areas. Their growing

Look for all the different ways children can and do express feelings.

command of language enables them to communicate their own feelings and to label the feelings and moods of others. Their developing capacity for independent decision making is evident as they make decisions and express preferences about people and relationships. Preschoolers actively seek out particular people to play with, talk to, and imitate; the friendships they develop often seem as close and complex as the relationships adults share with their own best friends.

As children's relationships develop, they include anger and tears as well as laughter and cooperation. The growing ability of preschoolers to gauge their own moods and those of others, plus their expanding language skills, provide a foundation for the development of social problem-solving skills. With adult support children can recognize issues involved in a conflict and can learn positive ways to express their needs and feelings. When adults encourage social problem solving, they are often surprised and delighted by children's ability to generate their own solutions to conflict situations.

As the teaching team discussed the play experiences that open this chapter, they recorded a variety of anecdotes. As the teachers discussed these incidents, they noted that many of children's behaviors reflected the High/Scope key experiences in **social relations and initiative.** In "Child Observations," pages 74–75, we list the nine key experiences in this category, and one or more of the child anecdotes that teachers linked to each key experience.

Supporting Children's Interest In People and Relationships

If we want to raise children to be responsible decision makers and social problem solvers, we need to give them the message, early in the preschool years, that they are capable of making decisions, solving problems, and taking responsibility. Imagine your own feelings if your friends and co-workers asked for your input but then continually disregarded or found fault with your ideas. In such circumstances, you would probably begin to doubt your abilities, even if you are usually self-assured. The same is true of children. If we want them to develop confidence in their abilities, we need to listen to, accept, and allow them to follow through on their ideas. Even when you think a child's idea won't work or the resulting activity may be too messy or loud, it's important to offer your support. Supporting children also means providing an environment where materials for carrying out their ideas are accessible and constantly maintained. Within such an environment, supportive adults play alongside children, showing them through their actions that they value what children are doing and saying. Adults must also be available to support children in resolving problems and conflicts, encouraging children to solve problems on their own and helping children generate new ideas when they can't come up with healthy and positive solutions independently.

The teachers who worked with the children in the opening examples used this supportive philosophy as they developed the following teaching strategies to support children's interests in baby and child care; games; and pets and pet shows.

Child Observations

INITIATIVE AND SOCIAL RELATIONS KEY EXPERIENCES

Making and expressing choices, plans, and decisions

When asked what her work time plan would be, Saraya said "house area." After she got there, she took all the baby dolls out of the crib and tossed them on the floor. Next she climbed inside the crib, sucked on her fingers, and said, "Waa, waa, waa."

At work time Alex came to the block area, where Daniel and Victor were building a dog house for Leah and Megan, and said, "Hey, let's have a dog show."

Solving problems encountered in play

At work time Audie was playing Old Maid with James and Erica. When Erica held her cards facing out, Audie said, "No, hold your cards the other way, so James can't see them."

At work time, Saraya removed the baby doll's clothes, left the doll on the table, and went to get a box of Kleenex. She used the Kleenex to swab at the doll's bottom, saying, "Ooh, you stink" as she wiped the doll.

Taking care of one's own needs

At work time Alex left the block area to collect paper, scissors, markers, and tape from the art area. He brought them back and then used the materials to make prize ribbons for the dog show.

At work time Saraya put the doll in the high chair, held it in with one hand, and stretched out the other hand to reach a necktie from the dress-up rack. She then tied the necktie around the baby doll and the back of the high chair.

Expressing feelings in words

At work time Saraya pretended to spoon cereal into the doll's mouth, saying "I like you better now."

At work time, while playing Old Maid with Audie and James, Erica said, "Oh, darn—I didn't get her," when she didn't succeed in picking the Old Maid Card.

General Teaching and Interaction Strategies

✔ **Express your interest in the ideas of children by positioning yourself at their physical levels, imitating their actions, and letting them take the lead in play.** Saraya's teacher followed this approach. While some adults might have been tempted to "teach" Saraya not to throw the baby dolls out of the bed onto the floor, this teacher showed her acceptance of Saraya's actions by simply sitting next to her, patting her back, and repeating her words. In the High/Scope approach we believe children need to deal with new situations in ways that make sense to them,

Participating in group routines

At work time Saraya (without being asked by another child or an adult) put the doll she had been playing with back in the bed before making a new plan to paint at the easel.

Being sensitive to the feelings, interests, and needs of others

At work time Alex leaned closer to Ashley, put his hand on her shoulder, and said, "There really wasn't anything else you could do." (Ashley had been explaining that she had to take a pretend trip to Florida with her doll babies because her husband had been drinking beer and had cursed at her.)

At work time Erica sat next to Audie and James as they played a game of Old Maid. When they finished she said, "Can I play this time?"

Building relationships with children and adults

At work time, after pretending to fly with her children to Florida, Ashley sat down next to an adult and described an argument she heard at her home the previous night.

As Daniel and Victor were building with blocks at work time, Megan and Leah crawled into the area and began barking at them.

Creating and experiencing collaborative play

At work time Daniel worked with Victor to reshape their block structure to enclose Megan and Leah. (The girls had come into their play area barking like dogs.) When Alex came over and suggested they put on a dog show with prize ribbons, Daniel helped him make the ribbons and suggested that the prizes go to "the loudest" and "the one that sleeps the most."

Dealing with social conflict

At work time Erica left a card game she was playing with Audie and James after both boys tried to give her instructions for playing the game (Erica hadn't been following the conventional rules). Before leaving she said, "Oh, brother."

and that teachers can best support this natural process by offering children the time and materials their actions tell us they need. When Saraya was ready, she later exhibited caring and nurturing interactions in her play with the baby dolls. The adult's patient, accepting attitude towards her earlier doll play helped Saraya reach this point.

✔ **Be a good listener.** Be cautious not to make judgments about the confidences children share in their play. When Ashley acted out an unpleasant incident she had apparently witnessed at home, the teacher did not suggest that Kevin was a bad person because he used harsh language and drank beer. Instead, she simply

By getting down on the floor with a child, the teacher communicates her interest in the child's play ideas.

reflected Ashley's words, hoping this would help Ashley feel secure enough to continue to share her troubling experiences in the future.

✔ **Always acknowledge the feelings children express,** whether they express them verbally or nonverbally. Don't try to talk children out of having feelings or downplay the importance of their feelings. Saying to Saraya "Don't cry—Mommy and Daddy had Lauren so you could have someone to play with" or "That baby bed is just for tiny babies, not big girls" would be insensitive to the inner turmoil she is feeling about her new position in the family.

✔ **Take children's developmental ages into consideration.** When Audie, James, and Erica were playing Old Maid, Erica's behavior showed she was not yet ready to play games with conventional rules. Understanding this, the teacher did not intervene and try to "teach" Erica the "correct" way to play. Instead she left the children to settle things for themselves, and Erica eventually decided that playing the game James and Audie's way was not for her.

✔ **Encourage children to solve the problems they encounter** while playing with objects and with others. Seeing that James and Audie were attempting to resolve their problem with Erica on their own, the teacher decided not to step in and mandate a solution. She let the incident take its own course. While James and Audie did not succeed in getting Erica to play the game their way, they were satisfied with her eventual decision to leave.

✔ **When working side by side with children, occasionally make suggestions that connect to their interests.** Since Alex's actions showed he had an understanding of the mechanics of a dog show, the teacher decided to wonder out loud if there would be different kinds of prize ribbons awarded. (After making her comment, she continued to play quietly with the materials Alex had brought.) As a result of her quiet, offhand comment, the children expanded their work and the teacher gained additional information about the abilities of Alex and Daniel.

✔ **Ask children for their suggestions on how to nurture others.** Alex's offer of comfort when Ashley talked about her reasons for going to Florida indicated he had ideas about how to care for others. If a new situation in which children needed understanding were to arise, the teacher might ask Alex what he thought they should do. This would give Alex another opportunity to sympathize and act as a model for other children.

Indoor and Outdoor Materials to Add

Baby and child care

1　If children in your classroom, like Saraya, have been imitating sucking infants, provide snack foods that require sucking. For example, teachers in Saraya's classroom offered frozen juice pops, cut-up orange sections, and drinks with straws as regular features on the snack menu.

2　Add real materials that adults might use in taking care of newborn children: a rocking chair, rattles, a bouncy seat, baby blankets, baby bottles, hooded towels, a plastic bathtub, a Snugli baby carrier, disposable diapers or cloth diapers with diaper wraps, diaper bags, empty rice cereal and formula containers, tiny spoons, and little plastic bowls.

3　To support children's interest in babies, add books about babies and caring for them to the book area, for example, *More, More, More, Said the Baby* by Vera B. Williams, *The New Baby* by Cyndy Szekeres, *Grover Takes Care of the Baby* by Emily Thompson, *Just Me and My Little Sister* by Mercer Mayer, and *The Baby's Catalog* by Janet and Allan Ahlberg. If children have been role-playing difficult family situations in their play, as Ashley did, you might also include some storybooks depicting families with problems. For example, *Daddy* by Jeannette Caines and *Mommy and Me by Ourselves Again* by Judith Vigna both portray children whose parents are separated.

Provide materials children can use to imitate baby care practices they see at home. Through such imitation children begin to develop the abilities needed to care for others.

Providing foods for sucking soon after the birth of a new sibling may help ease the child's transition.

4 To encourage children to solve problems as they play with baby-related materials, provide materials that offer built-in challenges. For example, offer a variety of baby bottles that have different-sized nipples and twist tops. Provide disposable diapers (which have closings that gradually lose their stickiness) so children have the opportunity to figure out new ways to hold the diapers in place.

Games

5 When children, like Audie and James, show you they are interested in games with rules, add simple board games (such as Candyland, Chutes and Ladders) and simple card games (Memory, Go Fish) to the toy area. Since, like Audie and James, many children are interested in playing games in pairs, be sure that some of the games you choose can be played by two people.

6 Choose computer games that children will enjoy playing cooperatively, in groups of two to four. For example, *The Playroom* from Broderbund Software and *Sammy's Science House* from Edmark Corporation work well with pairs and small groups of children.

7 Add a variety of small balls—for example, foam, hard plastic, or yarn balls—to the music area, then model their use in turn-taking games through your planning and recall strategies (see strategy 9, "Planning and Recall Experiences," page 81) and large-group time activities and games (see strategy 5, "Large-Group Experiences, page 84).

Pets and pet shows

8 Provide additional art supplies for making ribbons and other prizes. For example add used or blank award certificates, strips of satin and velvet ribbon, hole punches, string, and safety pins or paper clips to the art area.

Some materials lend themselves to cooperative play.

9 To encourage children to consider additional pet and award ideas, add related books to the book area, for example, *The Sesame Street Pet Show* by Emily Perl Kingsley.

Planning and Recall Experiences

Baby and child care

1 Swaddle a baby doll in a blanket and let children take turns describing their ideas to the baby as they rock or bounce the doll.

2 Ask children to pretend they are the mommy or daddy and you are the babysitter who is holding the baby. Ask the "parents" to talk about what they plan to do when they are gone or what they did when you were babysitting.

3 Using the rocking chair or baby bed as a prop, make up a chant or song (using a familiar tune) to indicate

If you learn that children play board games at home with their parents or siblings, add the same games to your toy area to give children the experience of using the games in a new setting.

A pretending game in which the parent (child) talks to the babysitter (teacher) is an engaging planning strategy. Erica gives the "babysitter" a detailed description of her work time plans.

whose turn it is to describe plans or experiences. For example:

> Tell us, tell us, what you will do (what you did) today.
> [Repeat two more times.]
> What will you do (what did you do) at work time?

4 With children sitting in a circle, have one person sit in the center and spin a baby bottle or rattle. The person the bottle/rattle points to when it stops spinning is the next to share plans or recall experiences.

5 Ask children to go to the interest areas to find one item they plan to use (or used) at work time. Children then put their item in a diaper bag. One person then pulls out the items one by one. As their items are picked, children describe their plans or experiences.

Games

6 Using heavy oak tag paper, make up a game board with a map of the different classroom areas. Have children indicate the interest area they plan to work in or

have worked in by putting a teddy bear counter in the appropriate space on the map.

7 To build on the turn-taking aspects of games, encourage children to take turns describing their plans (or work time activities) to one another. Break the group into pairs, place two chairs face to face for each pair, and ask children to sit facing their partners. Then ask children to find an item they plan to work with. After children have returned to their chairs with their toys and materials, have them take turns telling their plans or experiences to their partner with the item they plan to use (or did use) in hand.

Sharing a large piece of paper as they "write" or draw about their work time experiences is a recall time activity that supports children's newly emerging abilities to collaborate and communicate with others.

8 To build on older children's interest in card games such as Old Maid, bring a deck of cards to the planning or recall table. First give one card each to half the children at the table. Then have each child in the other half of the group pick a card from the matching set of cards in your hand. Have children find the child whose card matches theirs and then pair up with that person to plan or recall. On another day you could substitute pairs of socks or mittens for the matched pairs of cards. For older preschoolers you might use sets of items that go together but are not identical, for example, cup and saucer, diaper and doll, cassette tape and tape recorder, crayon and piece of paper.

9 To model new ideas for turn-taking games, sit with your group in a large circle on the floor. Provide a ball and ask children to roll, toss, or bounce it to the person who will be next to share ideas. Another turn-taking activity is a beanbag toss game in which each child shares a beanbag with a partner. The partners take turns throwing their beanbags into baskets labeled with interest area symbols, with children choosing the basket that represents the area where they plan to go or went during work time.

To follow up on Audie and James's interest in card-playing, the teacher has devised a card-matching game for planning time. The child whose card matches the next one picked is the next to plan.

Pets and pet shows

10 Using heavy paper and the strips of ribbon you added to the art area (see strategy 8, "Indoor and Outdoor Materials to Add," page 78), make area symbols that look like prize ribbons. Ask children to select the ribbon that stands for the area they plan to work in (or have worked in). Then have the children find ways to attach their ribbons to their clothing using tape, string, or pins.

11 Remind children who have been playing collaboratively of the partnerships they formed during play by asking children who are planning to play in the same area again, or who recall playing together, to discuss their plans or experiences together. For example, "Daniel, yesterday you made ribbons with Alex at work time. Will you work with him again today?" or "Megan and Leah, today at work time you were dogs. Can you tell the rest of the children what happened when you barked at Daniel and Victor?" As the children describe the details of their plans or experiences, encourage the whole group to act out their ideas by making appropriate motions.

12 To build on children's expanding awareness of feelings and their growing ability to solve the social problems that often arise during cooperative play experiences, at recall time encourage children to discuss an incident that involved feelings or the process of solving a social problem. For example, you might start recall time one day with "Peter, I heard you cry when Megan said you couldn't be a dog in the show. How did the two of you work out a solution to the problem?" Listen carefully as the child describes in his own words the incident and the outcome.

Small-Group Experiences

Baby and child care

1 To encourage children to express feelings in words use small-group time to design a card for a child, like Saraya, whose family situation has changed. Provide materials for card-making and start by saying something like "Today I brought some materials you can use if you'd like to make a picture or write a story for Saraya about her new sister." Observe which children use the materials for exploration, which actually make something for the child in question, and which write or dictate messages for their cards or pictures. Consider your observations in terms of children's developing representational and literacy abilities. When teachers tried this strategy in Saraya's classroom, the children responded with several memorable creations. Megan, after drawing herself with her new brother, asked her teacher to write, "I have a baby and some days it's not a pretty picture." Jack, whose own mother was pregnant at the time, had the teacher write this message on his drawing, "I hope it's a brother and if it's a sister I'm going to blast her up to the sky."

2 Set out bathing containers, gentle soap, baby washcloths, towels, clothing, and dolls. Watch to see which children bathe and dress the dolls.

Games

3 Bring several decks of cards to the table and explain that some children like to play matching games with cards. Ask children for their ideas about different ways cards can be used and then observe which children use them for stacking, shuffling, building, matching, flipping, and so forth. As you observe individual children you will probably gain information on their spatial, classification, and fine-motor skills.

Pets and pet shows

4 If you have observed children playing collaboratively as they did in the pet show example, support further relationship-building by offering materials that encourage sharing and working toward a common goal. Provide an over-sized Lego base, for example, to encourage pairs of children to build together, and in the process, to converse and negotiate. Another idea is to set out several larger-than-usual baskets of crayons rather than one basket for each child at the table; if you do this, make sure each basket is positioned so several children can reach into it. A variation of the crayon idea that you might try on another day is to put two cups each of three different-colored tempera paints on the table.

5 Think of something else in your class that needs to be cared for and enlist the help of your group in devising a solution. In one class, the teacher took the children to the block area and told them the hermit crab needed exercise but couldn't be out in the large space without some kind of enclosure. Children then worked together, using blocks, to design a safe and spacious enclosure for the crabs.

Large-Group Experiences

Baby and child care

1 If children have been engaging in baby-related play, have the group act out various aspects of baby care, such as rocking, bouncing, feeding, burping, diaper-changing, singing, and bathing. Give children the opportunity to suggest both the activity and the accompanying motions.

2 Sing variations of familiar songs that depict baby-related themes and encourage children to use words to label feelings. For example, the song "If You're Happy and You Know It" might be changed to "If You're a Baby and You're [feeling word]." The new words are as follows:

> If you're a baby and you're SAD,
> Cry so loud (Waa, Waa).
> [Repeat first two lines]
> If you're a baby and you're sad,
> Then your life will surely show it,
> [Repeat first two lines.]

Make up new verses that incorporate feeling words and actions suggested by children. For example, "If you're a baby and you're happy, kick your legs [Children kick legs.]"

3 Ask children to form two lines so they are positioned far apart and facing each other. Have each child select a doll or stuffed animal. Then give the first person in each line a baby stroller or carriage. Have that person put their animal or doll in the stroller and push it across the space to the other line and back, handing the stroller, in relay-race fashion, to the next person in line.

Games

4 To build on children's interest in the turn-taking aspect of games, sing familiar games or chants such as "Who Took the Cookie From the Cookie Jar?," giving individual children the opportunity to choose the next person to complete the chant. Develop your own variations on the songs or chants based on children's actions in the classroom. For example, in Audie, Erica, and James's classroom, teachers developed this variation, chanting the words in a steady beat:

> Who took a card from the Old Maid game?
> Audie took a card from the Old Maid game.
> [Audie responds] "Who me? Not me. Couldn't be.
> Erica took a card from the Old Maid game."
> [Erica responds] "Who me? Not me. Couldn't be.
> James took a card from the Old Maid game."
> [Repeat.]

5 As a way of helping children make the transition from large-group time to the next activity, roll a foam or yarn ball to a child, and suggest that the child be the first person to leave the activity. Before moving to the next activity, the child selected rolls the ball to the next child to leave, and so on.

Pets and pet shows

6 Ask children to name a pet and a title it might win at a pet show, for example, the dog who is the loudest barker, cat with the softest fur, squirrel who is the fastest nibbler. After a child shares an idea, the group acts it out.

What We Learned From Our Observations of Children

In this chapter we've looked at some of the ways children explore feelings and relationships through pretend play and play with simple games. While children use the full range of their developing abilities in such social play experiences, these kinds of play offer especially good opportunities for observing children's developing skills in social relations and initiative. Teachers often find that the sections of the High/Scope Child Observation Record (COR) dealing with **initiative** and **social relations** are a useful tool for interpreting their observations of children's social play. Within any group, teachers will find that children are at varying developmental levels on particular COR items such as *engaging in complex play, relating to adults,* and *making friends with other children.* The COR helps teachers identify children's specific abilities in such areas and plan interaction strategies and experiences that will encourage children to use and expand these abilities. On pages 86–87 we show some of the anecdotal notes teachers recorded as they observed children, both during the play incidents that open this chapter and during the play experiences that resulted when the suggested teaching strategies were tried in the classroom. Each anecdote is matched with a corresponding COR item and level from the **initiative** or **social relations** sections. To illustrate varying levels of development within particular COR items, two or three anecdotes per item are given.

Collaborative play may often be observed in or near the block area.

Children play with hermit crabs after cooperating in designing an enclosure for them.

The computer area is another common center for social play.

Child Observations

INITIATIVE

Teacher's Anecdotal Notes	*High/Scope COR Item and Level*
When asked for her work time plan, Megan said, "to be a dog again."	A. Expressing choices: (3) Child indicates desired activity, place of activity, materials, or playmates with a short sentence.
At planning time, Frances told her planning partner—"I'm going to play Old Maid, but only by myself."	A. Expressing choices: (4) Child indicates with a short sentence how plans will be carried out.
"I'm making a picture of me and Daniel [her new baby brother] and then I want you to write on it for me," said Megan to Carol [her teacher].	A. Expressing choices: (4) Child indicates with a short sentence how plans will be carried out.
At work time Kayla brought the tape container from the art area and put a piece of tape on each side of a disposable diaper to fasten the diaper on the doll.	B. Solving problems: (3) Child uses one method to try to solve a problem, but if unsuccessful, gives up after one or two tries.
At small-group time, Ruthi tried three times to balance cards in an upright position, then said, "That doesn't work." Then she got two blocks and set a card against each one to "make a tunnel." Finally, she moved the blocks closer together and made a ceiling for the tunnel with a third card.	B. Solving problems: (5) Child tries alternative methods to solve a problem and is highly involved and persistent.
At work time Megan stayed in her pretend-dog role for 10 minutes, remaining inside her wooden enclosure and barking.	C. Engaging in complex play: (2) Child shows interest in simple use of materials or simple participation in activities.
At work time Ashley went to the house area, packed a flight bag with child and doll clothing, and took it with two baby dolls to the block area. There she pretended to board a plane for Florida (sitting down for a moment on a block), then left with her belongings and moved to the book area, where she pretended she was in Florida.	C. Engaging in complex play: (4) Child, acting alone, carries out complex and varied sequences of activities.
James got out the Go Fish cards, divided them into thirds to provide a "Go Fish" pile and sets for him and Audie, then played the game with Audie for 10 minutes, following the conventional rules.	C. Engaging in complex play: (5) Child joins with others in carrying out complex and varied sequences of activities.
At the end of small-group time Jonah came back to the block area and put the last three blocks back on the shelf before going outside.	D. Cooperating in program routines: (4) Child participates in program routines without being asked.
At planning time when Carol [a teacher] took a moment to greet a late-arriving family, Melissa said, "O.K., Frederick, you hold the baby next and tell everybody what your plan is for today."	D. Cooperating in program routines: (5) Child continues program routines even when an adult is not nearby.

SOCIAL RELATIONS

TEACHER'S ANECDOTAL NOTES	*HIGH/SCOPE COR ITEM AND LEVEL*
At work time, referring to the Old Maid game he had played, James said to Carol [his teacher], "We played with Erica but she doesn't know how yet."	E. Relating to adults: (3) Child initiates interactions with familiar adults.
At outside time Megan asked Leah's nanny to go on a walk with her and her baby. They spent 15 minutes strolling around the playground together. As they walked, Megan pushed the baby carriage, stopping to look at the daffodils and the freshly planted grass seed.	E. Relating to adults: (4) Child sustains interactions with familiar adults.
Leah responded to Megan's plan ("play with Leah and make a ribbon") by walking hand in hand with Megan to the art area.	F. Relating to other children: (2) Child responds when other children initiate interactions.
Daniel worked with Victor, using the large, hollow blocks to make a dog house to enclose Megan and Leah, then worked with Alex to create prize ribbons for a dog show.	F. Relating to other children: (5) Child works on complex projects with other children.
At work time, after completing one move in the **Sammy's Science House** computer game, Kacey handed the computer mouse to Julia, explaining that she was doing this ". . . because you're my best friend."	G. Making friends with other children: (3) Child identifies a classmate as a friend.
At work time Alex leaned closer to Ashley, put his hand on her shoulder and said, "There really wasn't anything else you could do," after she talked about taking her babies away from home because of the harsh language and drinking that had occurred.	G. Making friends with other children: (5) Child appears to receive social support from a friend and shows loyalty to the friend.
At work time, when Sue pulled a doll out of Saraya's hand, Tanuka said, "No, Sue. Look at her face. You made her cry. Now give it back and wait your turn."	H. Engaging in social problem solving: (4) Child sometimes attempts to solve problems with other children independently, by negotiation or other socially acceptable means.
While playing Old Maid with Erica, Audie told her, "No, hold your cards the other way so James can't see them." He also said, "You're supposed to try NOT to get the Old Maid."	H. Engaging in social problem solving: (4) Child sometimes attempts to solve problems with other children independently, by negotiation or other socially acceptable means.
Sue grabbed a doll Saraya had been holding, and when Tanuka told her to give it back and wait her turn Sue said, "No, I don't have to, 'cause you're not my boss."	I. Understanding and expressing feelings: (2) Child expresses or verbalizes feelings, but sometimes in unacceptable ways.
Michael put his arm around Saraya and rocked the baby bed back and forth while she was lying inside it at work time.	I. Understanding and expressing feelings: (5) Child responds appropriately to the feelings of others.

Adult Training Activities

To highlight the relationship between classroom activities and the **key experiences in initiative and social relations,** have participants match the appropriate key experiences to the anecdotes that follow, writing the number of the key experience in the space provided. Participants may work by themselves or with partners.

Initiative and Social Relations Key Experiences

1. Making and expressing choices, plans, and decisions

2. Solving problems encountered in play

3. Taking care of one's own needs

4. Expressing feelings in words

5. Participating in group routines

6. Being sensitive to the feelings, interests, and needs of others

7. Building relationships with children and adults

8. Creating and experiencing collaborative play

9. Dealing with social conflict

Play Anecdotes

_____ *Victor and Daniel were building a dog show stage together when Daniel accidentally knocked down part of the stage. Victor pushed him, saying "Get out!"*

_____ *"I can help Kayla tape the diaper," said Mark.*

_____ *Audrey turned on the computer, selected **The Playroom** program, and said, "Hey, does anyone want to play with me?"*

_____ *Madison showed Victor a baby bottle and said, "I'm going to feed my baby before you babysit him."*

_____ *At work time, James built a maze for the hermit crab and then asked his teacher for help in getting the crab out of its cage.*

_____ *Audie and Donald took turns pushing and riding in the baby stroller. When it was Donald's turn to ride, Donald said, "Push me faster, Audie. I like this!"*

_____ *"I feel sad when Mommy cries in her room," said Ashley to Madison.*

_____ *Hannah tried putting the diaper wrap on the baby doll backwards. When it fell off, she tied the doll down again and asked Kayla to hold the baby's legs up. Then she pulled the wrap in between the doll's legs, and fastened the Velcro closings.*

_____ *After Ashley recalled her pretend trip to Florida, Alex asked her, "Are you feeling better now?"*

Celebrations 6

Experiencing

Holidays and

Special Events

G raham, whose mother is expecting a second child in three weeks, makes a plan
to work in the art area. When he gets there, he collects tape, markers, and
newspaper and takes the materials to the house area. Graham gets a baby rattle,
a diaper wrap, and a board book and wraps them inside the newspaper. Then he
takes a doll, puts it under his shirt, and sits on a chair next to the wrapped present.
"I'm having the shower. Bring me presents and put them over here," he says to
his teacher.

※

"How was your weekend?" the teacher asks Donald on Monday morning as he
arrives with his mother. Donald launches into a description of a citywide art fair he
attended where he watched an artist "pour some stuff over a lady's face." Continuing
his story, Donald relates that the lady "had two straws coming out of her nose and
one coming out of her mouth so she could breathe." As Donald describes his experience, his mother smiles. She explains that they saw an artist covering a woman's
face with plaster to make a face mask and that the artist had indeed used straws to
enable the woman to breathe.

　　Later that morning at snack time, Donald tells Kelly about going to the art
fair: "I saw Jingles the Clown with her potbelly pig, Wilbur. I touched him and he
was scratchy." He also tells Kelly that a different clown made a blue dog for him
out of a balloon and that "it was very crowded and hot and I got grouchy." He then
explains how his dad said he could cool off by "sitting down on the grass to listen to

music." When his teacher asked what kind of music he listened to, he said, "People standing up with drums and other people dancing right in the street."

@

*It is the middle of February. The teacher is greeting children and their parents as they arrive at school. Natasha takes off her coat. She is wearing pink tights and a pink ballerina dress. She hands the teacher a brown paper bag and says, "Here, will you put my wings on? They go in the back." Her father explains to the teacher that when Natasha woke up and asked to wear her Halloween costume, he at first said no, pointing out that Halloween was over. However, when she persisted, he said she could wear the costume to school if it was all right with her teacher. The teacher helps Natasha fasten her wings onto her back, and Natasha sits down to read with the other children at greeting time. At the end of greeting time the teacher asks if all the children can "flutter their wings over to the planning tables." When Adriana asks, "What means **flutter**?" Natasha jumps up, spreads out her arms, moves them up and down, and tiptoes to her planning table. When she gets there she turns around and says, "**That** means **flutter.**" Natasha's Halloween pretending continues at work time, as she and other children pretend to go trick-or-treating.*

@

Later that same week in February, Brianna brings a box of Valentine cards from home. Her mother explains to the teacher that Brianna's older sister has been addressing Valentine cards for her friends in the evenings and that Brianna has been wanting to do the same. "Brianna wouldn't stop bugging me about this," the mother says, explaining that she finally decided to get Brianna her own box of cards. At work time that day Brianna gets a large block and sets it up to use as a table. She spreads her Valentine cards out in front of the table and writes her name and personal symbol on the back of each one. Martin sits down next to her and asks her what she is doing. "Making cards for my friends," she replies.

Celebrating With Children: Taking the Child's Point of View

Children are sensitive to changes in their environment, so it's not surprising that they respond to the bustle and excitement that surrounds holidays, community events, birthdays, and other special occasions. Before and after a special event, children enjoy talking about an event or re-enacting it in pretend play; they also enjoy making event-related objects and materials—cards, presents, decorations, special foods.

As with any other play topic or activity that is of interest to children, adults in High/Scope settings support children's interest in special occasions by using appropriate interaction strategies and offering related experiences and materials. In so doing, however, it's important for adults to remember that preschoolers do not experience these special events as adults do.

First, keep in mind that preschool children are interested in special events that involve activities and materials they can *directly experience*. For example, preschoolers typically enjoy and remember activities like opening up presents, dressing in costumes, or listening to music in a street that is normally filled with cars. On the other hand, they are unlikely to understand historic and traditional aspects of holidays that are remote from their everyday experiences. Holidays such as Columbus Day and President's Day may not seem as real to preschool children because they are usually not tied to specific experiences in their lives. Such holidays are often more meaningful to grade-school children, who can begin to understand the historical significance of such occasions.

Another thing to keep in mind as you plan around special occasions and holidays is the preschooler's need for consistency. However excited you are about an upcoming special event, it's important to resist the urge to change the routine that has been established in your classroom and is familiar to the children. Holidays or special occasions often bring with them a change in children's home routines. Extra family members arrive, special foods are eaten, interaction patterns change, and bedtimes are altered. In the eyes of a child, such changes may be scary or confusing. However, in the preschool environment, you can support children's need for consistency by maintaining your routine and physical setting. Instead of shifting your schedule around, plan your special-occasion activities so they occur during regular parts of the routine, such as small-group, large-group, and outside times. For example, Graham's teachers used daily greeting time and the message board that was used for everyday announcements to announce the special baby shower party that was held at Graham's house (see strategy 3, large-group experiences, page 101). Similarly, when you are adding special-occasion materials to the classroom, incorporate them in the regular interest areas, and when appropriate, introduce them to children at small-group time or greeting time. When you maintain a consistent physical setting and schedule, even when introducing new materials or experiences, preschoolers experience their environment as one that they understand and have control over.

In planning around special events, it's also important to remember that children experience holidays on their own personal timetables. Their interest in a holiday depends

After Halloween, children enjoy face-painting with markers.

on their own perceptions, experiences, and fantasies; it may not correspond to a calendar date. By contrast, the adult approach to special occasions is typically calender-oriented. In many preschool settings, adults who are caught up in their own excitement about an approaching holiday begin preparations long before the actual holiday date. The activities they plan for small-group time, the songs they choose for large-group time, and the decorations and craft materials they add to the physical environment all reflect the approaching celebration. Then, the day after the holiday, adults remove the special materials from the classroom and start a new cycle of activities reflecting the next holiday on the calendar. However, just as all signs of the holiday are disappearing from the classroom, the children's interest in the special event may actually be at its highest. This is because special events often do not become real to children until after they occur. The children's interest in holiday-related play and activities often continues long after the event is over. And even when children's interest in a special event seems to have subsided, for some children it sometimes resurfaces again, weeks or months after the actual event.

As Natasha's request for a Halloween costume in February so clearly shows, nothing is more important to children than the present, than what they are interested in "right now." Preschool children are still developing concepts of the past and the future, and the notion of calendar time is usually far beyond their understanding. To celebrate special occasions in ways that are meaningful to children, then, it is important for adults to take into account how preschoolers understand time.

Preschool children may also differ from adults in their ideas about the content of holiday activities or the aspects of the special event that are important to them. While adults have years of experience with traditions and rituals associated with special occasions, children approach them with a fresh perspective that is shaped by their personal interests and family experiences. It's important to remember that families differ in their ways of observing special occasions and holidays. Not everyone celebrates the same occasions and holidays, and even when they do, they rarely observe them in the same ways. These differences in children's interests and family experiences will be reflected in their holiday-related activities.

These children recently visited an outdoor festival where they saw a clown on stilts and a trapeze artist walking a tightrope. Back in the classroom Linda prepares her own stilts and Chris walks the tightrope with his teacher's help.

The only way to understand what captures a child's interest in an event is to observe and listen to the child. For example, 4-year-old Olga's Ukrainian family celebrated Easter by preparing a special braided bread. A few days after Easter, Olga's teachers observed her making her own version of Easter bread in the classroom by braiding Play-Doh strips and carefully placing them on top of a mound of Play-Doh. Though this way of celebrating Easter was very important to Olga, it was a new experience for her teachers.

Supporting Children's Interest in Special Occasions and Holidays

Because children approach special events in individual ways, it is extremely important that adults utilize all their observational powers in developing strategies that are meaningful to children. Your observations of children's conversations and actions will tell you a great deal about their understanding of and involvement in special celebrations and will guide you in developing appropriate support strategies.

In responding to Donald's street-fair experience, Graham's baby shower, Brianna's interest in valentines, and Natasha's February Halloween, the teachers developed the support strategies presented in the pages that follow. In developing these strategies they not only focused on the specific aspects of the events that interested children but also on the particular key experiences they noticed in children's special-event-related play. On pages 94–95 is a selection of anecdotes the teaching team recorded as they discussed these children's experiences. The notes are grouped according to the High/Scope key experience categories.

General Teaching and Interaction Strategies

✔ **When interacting with children as they enact and represent holiday and special-occasion experiences through play, strive to recognize and react appropriately to the *child's* definition of the special occasion.** Rather than imposing on children your own notions about a special occasion, wait until the event comes up in children's play and respond by incorporating the child's ideas. For example, when Olga was making braided "Easter bread" out of Play-Doh, her teacher worked alongside her, making a similar loaf, even though the teacher's own personal Easter memories involved Easter baskets and bunnies. Similarly, when Graham invited his teacher to attend the pretend baby shower he was planning, the teacher based her actions on Graham's own enactment of the occasion. She told Graham she would be coming as soon as she wrapped a present for the baby and, just as she had seen Graham do a few moments earlier, she selected a board book from the book shelf and wrapped it in newspaper. Then she joined Graham's play by placing the present in the place he had suggested. As she was wrapping the book, she told Carleen, who was working next to her at the art table, that she was wrapping a present for Graham's baby shower. A few minutes later, the teacher noticed Carleen wrapping her own gift to bring.

Child Observations

CREATIVE REPRESENTATION

At work time Graham put a doll under his shirt, sat on a chair next to a present he had wrapped, and said, "I'm having the shower."

LANGUAGE AND LITERACY

At snack, when asked to describe music he listened to at the art fair, Donald said, "People standing up with drums and other people dancing right in the street."

Brianna spent all of work time preparing Valentine cards for her friends. She put her name and symbol on the back of each of her Valentine cards.

INITIATIVE AND SOCIAL RELATIONS

At work time Graham arranged the setting for a pretend baby shower in the house area. Then he said to Beth [a teacher], "Bring me presents and put them over here."

At work time, when Martin asked Brianna what she was doing she answered, "Making cards for my friends."

MOVEMENT

At the suggestion "Let's all flutter to the planning table," Natasha stretched out her arms to the sides and flapped them up and down while tiptoeing to the planning area.

MUSIC

At work time Natasha got a paper bag from the art area, knocked on the opening to the house area, and chanted, "Trick or treat, trick or treat, give me something good to eat."

✔ **Be sensitive to the fact that children's memories of special occasions may arise at any time,** even months after the event. We should support children whenever they choose to re-enact an experience, regardless of whether the time seems appropriate. If children, like Natasha, are pretending to trick-or-treat in February, join in their play rather than attempt to discourage them because Halloween is over.

✔ **Expect that some children will show little or no interest at all in a holiday celebration** that excites you and the other children in the class. For example, in the preschool classroom described in this chapter, some children were not at all interested in making valentines with Brianna or trick-or-treating with Natasha. In these cases, the teachers simply observed these children's interests and play ideas and used appropriate interaction strategies to support them.

✔ **Some children may even express concern and fear about holiday-related activities; in such cases acknowledge the child's feelings and support them in finding a more comfortable activity.** When Natasha pretended to trick-or-treat, Carleen

CLASSIFICATION

At work time Graham selected three items to wrap for his baby shower present: a baby rattle, a diaper wrap, and a board book.

SERIATION

At work time as Natasha twirled around in her ballerina costume, Emma said to her, "My ballerina music box goes fast, faster, fastest."

NUMBER

At greeting time Donald said that a lady at the art fair had "two straws coming out of her nose and one straw out of her mouth."

SPACE

At the beginning of work time Natasha asked Carol [a teacher] for help in putting on ballerina wings, saying "They go in the back." Later, when the five-minute warning was announced, Natasha went up to Carol and said, "Take off my wings. I'll do the rest."

TIME

At work time after opening the baby shower "present," Graham got up from his chair and said, "Okay, now it's time to start the eating."

ran to a teacher and said, "I'm scared of Halloween. I don't like it. Tell her to stop." The teacher responded by saying "Halloween is pretty scary" and stayed with Carleen until she was engrossed in another activity. The teacher's words and actions supported Carleen's way of labeling what she was experiencing and let Carleen know the teacher recognized and empathized with her feelings.

✔ **Show children, through your actions, that you are really listening to their descriptions of the special events they have experienced.** When Donald talked about sitting in the grass and listening to people playing drums at the street fair, the teacher stood and moved her hands up and down as if she were pounding on a set of drums. "Is this what the drummers looked like, Donald?" she asked. "No, the drums were lower" was his response.

✔ **Whenever possible, incorporate children's spontaneous recollections of holidays and special occasions in classroom activities, even when this means changing an activity you have planned.** Natasha's teacher did this when she asked the children

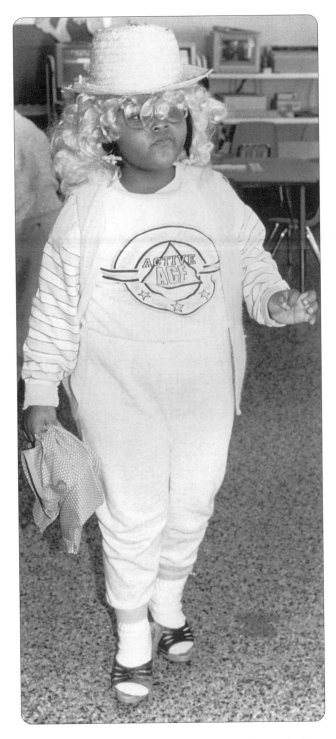

Don't be surprised when children pretend it's Halloween in the middle of February.

if they could "flutter like butterflies" to the planning table. The teacher had not known that Natasha would arrive at school in costume and had in fact been planning to use a different strategy for the transition to planning.

Indoor and Outdoor Materials to Add

Baby shower

1 If children have been re-enacting family celebrations, add to the art area wrapping paper, streamers, ribbons, and the fronts of used greeting cards appropriate to special occasions that individual children have talked about and enacted.

2 After children have been involved in a pretend baby shower, add appropriate items to the house area. Graham's teachers added baby items similar to the gifts the family received at the shower for his brother: board books, rattles, blankets, diapers, a fold-up stroller, and a bassinet.

Street fair

3 After children in your group have attended a street fair, encourage children to build their own pretend booth displays by adding building materials to your classroom. Donald's teachers added long pieces of wood, hammers, safety goggles, and nails to the classroom construction area. (By this time, the teachers had already taken the entire class on a field trip to the same art fair Donald had attended. During the trip, the children had watched artists and their helpers constructing the booths).

4 For outside time or small-group time, set up your own outdoor street art fair using large traffic cones to set off the street fair area from the rest of the playground. Behind the cones, set up large cardboard boxes on end and decorate the insides with children's art works. You might also add a platform equipped with musical instruments and microphones (to serve as a stage for musical performances), a cash box with play money so children can buy and sell their art, and a snack booth with real or toy food. Bring a tape recorder or radio outside to provide music for the performers and street dancers. Be sure to leave your street fair set up at the end of the day so parents can stroll through it with their children.

Holidays

5 To build on children's interest in wearing Halloween costumes and to help allay the concerns of children who find Halloween scary, add mask-making materials and washable face paint to the art area. (If you have computers, you might also add a computer program such as *Mask Parade* from Queue, Inc.) Seeing others painting faces and making masks may help some children who are afraid of people in costumes to see that there are familiar people behind the disguises. Note, however, that some children may still be frightened; in this case, respond appropriately to their concerns.

6 Take photos of children in their costumes at your classroom Halloween celebration. If children re-enact Halloween later in the year, put some costumes in the house area that are similar to the ones children wore at Halloween. Also include trick-or-treat bags and flashlights.

7 Collect the fronts of valentines and other holiday cards and add them to the art area. Store them near a container of different-sized envelopes. Inside the container of envelopes, you might also include a class list with children's names and symbols. After Brianna's teachers tried this strategy, Brianna spent several work times copying children's symbols and the letters of their names onto the cards and envelopes available in the art area.

8 Collect newspaper advertising supplements describing holiday-related products and add them to your book or art area. Put holiday-related books out on bookshelves. Again, respond to children's interests even if the holiday is over. In response to Natasha's trick-or-treating, for example, teachers brought several Halloween books out of storage and put them back on book shelves.

9 Cut the fronts of holiday cards in half. Store them in a container and put them on the toy area shelf. Children can match the picture halves or make silly new cards by mismatching the halves.

Equip your classroom with card-making materials so children can make cards to express holiday greetings (or any other personal feeling) at any time.

10 Add a real mailbox near the exit or entrance to the classroom and watch to see if children use the mailbox to "mail" the greeting cards they've made or chosen.

Planning and Recall Experiences

Baby shower

1 To re-enact a baby shower a child has told you about, hold a planning or recall "party." Arrange your planning/recall space to simulate a gift table with a chair next to it. Ask children to get a material they plan to use (or used) at work time and to place it on the table. Then have children take turns pretending to be the "mommy" who is receiving the baby gifts. The mommy chooses one item and tries to guess who plans to use the item (or who used the item) at work time. After the guess is made, the child who was named describes his or her plans or experiences.

2 To support children's interest in wrapping and opening presents, wrap items from each of the classroom areas in newspaper, put them in a large shopping bag, and bring them to the planning/recall table. At planning time, ask one child at a time to pick a "present" out of the bag, open it, and ask the others, "Will anybody use this?" Then have any children who say yes discuss their plans to use that object. At recall time, ask a child who did not get a chance to unwrap a present at planning time to choose one of the remaining "presents" and find out if anyone used that item during their work time activities. Continue with the same process until all presents are unwrapped and all children have described their experiences.

Street fair

3 To simulate outdoor performances children have seen at a street fair, have the group sit outside on the grass or on make-believe grass somewhere in the classroom. Provide a drum or an area for dancing so the person planning or recalling can beat the drum or dance while describing their work time plans or experiences.

4 Set up a miniature street fair on the planning/recall table, making "booths" out of small blocks and placing an interest area symbol card within each one. Give each child a little plastic person or a teddy bear counter to walk to the "booth" representing the play area of his or her choice.

5 Have children tell their plans or experiences to a special person, character, or animal they saw at the street fair. For example, to follow up on Donald's description of the "potbelly pig," teachers brought a plastic pig to the planning/recall table and asked children to tell their plans or experiences to "Wilbur."

Holidays

6 Bring to the planning/recall area a prop that represents the holiday children are celebrating. (Natasha and Brianna's teachers used a ballerina doll and a valentine card.) Ask children to take turns holding the prop and sharing plans or experiences.

7 Make ballerina wings and ask the person who is planning or recalling to put them on and then to "flutter" to his or her chosen play area. The rest of the

Leave materials in your classroom interest areas that remind children of holiday experiences.

children follow, also pretending to flutter by waving their arms to simulate wing motions. The children take turns wearing the wings, leading the group to new areas, and describing their plans or experiences.

8 Provide personalized Valentine cards for the children in the group with a different child's name and symbol written on the back of each one. Place the cards in a bag and then pick one; the person whose card is chosen is the next to share plans or experiences.

Small-Group Experiences

Baby shower

1 Bake or cook a special dish or treat as a gift for a family in the class who is celebrating a family event. After Graham's family held the baby shower, the children baked blueberry muffins for his family.

2. Ask family members what food items were served at a recent family celebration and prepare a similar treat or dish with the small group. The day after the baby shower for Graham's mother, the teacher provided fruit and blunt knives for her small group. Children peeled bananas and cut up the fruit to make a fruit salad. Graham's parents had donated the leftover baby shower napkins, paper bowls, and decorations; these additional reminders of the shower experience were used when the fruit salad was served in the small group.

3. Ask parents to donate wrapping paper, gift boxes, gift tags, and bows from home gift-giving celebrations. Provide tape, scissors, and markers to be used with these materials, and make the materials available in a special place so children can explore gift-wrapping.

Street fair

4. Provide materials so children can re-enact their experiences of seeing artists create things at a street fair. To help children re-enact Donald's experience of watching an artist make a plaster mask of a woman's face, Donald's teachers provided straws, modeling clay, and Play-Doh, along with materials for making imprints in the clay—doll babies, dinosaurs, and plastic animals.

5. To broaden children's understanding of a street fair, give children an opportunity to see structures for the fair being set up or taken down. Donald's teacher took the class on a field trip to the art-fair site, timing their arrival so children could watch the artists setting up their booths for the day. They might also have arranged the trip for late in the day, so children could watch as booths were disassembled and streets were cleared of art-fair debris.

6. If children have had an opportunity to watch the construction or disassembly of street-fair structures, provide materials so they can re-enact these activities. After children watched artists building their display spaces, Donald's teachers provided hammers, nails, and pieces of wood for an outdoor small-group time experience. If children have watched workers cleaning up the street and sidewalks after a fair, you might provide brooms, brushes, and large garbage bags for tidying up the school yard and sidewalks.

Holidays

7. Provide materials so children can design their own special-occasion greeting cards: oak tag paper, pre-cut pictures, stickers, markers, glue, and so forth. Assist children in writing their own messages on their cards in their own ways. Accept and encourage all forms of children's writing, including scribbles, letterlike forms, invented spelling, and conventional letters and words, and be available to write down children's dictated messages. Do not push children to make cards if they are not interested, and avoid imposing on children your own notions of proper card-exchange customs.

8 Repeat the previous strategy on another day, this time also providing envelopes and stamps (the picture stamps that come as advertisements for ordering magazines work well).

Large-Group Experiences

Baby shower

1 Wrap five or six baby items in newspaper and set them in the middle of the large-group space. As children take turns unwrapping "presents," make up songs about how the gift items will be used. For example, sing (to the tune of "Here We Go 'Round the Mulberry Bush"):

> This is the way you read a book,
> Read a book, read a book,
> This is the way you read a book,
> When you have a baby.

Depending on the baby items you have, other verses might include, "This is the way you push the stroller," ". . . change a diaper," ". . . hold the bottle."

2 Make up songs or fingerplays that use children's own words and actions to describe special-occasion events and classroom re-enactments of these events. After the fruit salad snack, children made up the following song to the tune of "Ten Little Indians" (the words suggested by children are bold-faced):

> One little, two little, three little **banana slices,**
> Four little, five little, six little **blueberries,**
> Seven little, eight little, nine little **apple chunks,**
> Ten little **ras-ber-ries.**

As they sang this song, children pantomimed the motions of cutting up fruit and putting it in the salad bowl.

3 Incorporate children's announcements of special events into the part of the routine in which classroom announcements are ordinarily shared with the group as a whole, for example, at the beginning of large-group time or at greeting time. In Graham's classroom, announcements are shared at greeting time using a message board on which messages are posted in picture-writing. On the day after the baby shower, the message board included the announcement that there had been a baby shower at Graham's house. The pictorial message included Graham's symbol and

"I made a birthday card for my Mom," says Trey, "because tonight's the day we'll have the cake."

simple drawings of a house and a woman with a large belly. As the class discussed the message, Graham provided additional details about the occasion. The message board was also used to announce the baby-shower materials that were added to the classroom; included on the board were small pictures of baby rattles, diapers, board books, and a baby bassinet.

Street fair

4 Play a recorded selection in the same musical style as performances children heard at a street fair (for example, steel-drum music or Dixieland jazz) and provide materials for drumming, such as wood blocks and sticks. Play the music and encourage children to beat the drum or dance to the beat.

5 Follow up on children's descriptions of their street-fair experiences by asking children to pantomime them. At large-group time, the teachers asked Donald to show everyone how the "pot-belly pig" moved when it walked. Then they encouraged the other children to imitate Donald's actions. Next they asked the children to suggest additional animal movements for the group to imitate.

Holidays

6 Introduce children to traditional holiday songs and fingerplays when their actions suggest, as Brianna's did, that they are interested in the event. In this traditional Valentine fingerplay, children take turns inserting the names of their friends:

> One little valentine said, "I love you."
> _____made another, then there were two.
> Two little valentines, one for me.
> _____made another, then there were three.
> Three little valentines said, "We need one more."
> _____made another, then there were four.
> Four little valentines, one more to arrive.
> _____made another, then there were five.
> Five little valentines all ready to say,
> "Be my Valentine on this happy day."

7 Don't be concerned if children's interest in holiday songs or games doesn't correspond to the calendar. You may not expect to sing "Jingle Bells" in January, but if that is children's interest, support it. If interest in a holiday re-emerges weeks or months after the actual event, re-introduce related songs and games at large-group time. For example, on the day that Natasha came to school in her Halloween costume, teachers re-introduced a favorite Halloween fingerplay. They also devised a Halloween-related game for ending large-group time. As a child left the group to go to the next activity, he or she chose the next child to leave by tapping that child on the shoulder, chanting "Trick or treat, it's time to leave, I'm knocking at your door."

What We Learned From Our Observations of Children

After implementing the teaching strategies in this chapter, adults observed and documented a wide range of learning experiences. Their anecdotal notes on these experiences highlight some of the things teachers learned about the children during these play incidents. A sampling of these notes is given in "Child Observations" on the next three pages. Each anecdote is keyed to a corresponding item in the High/Scope Child Observation Record (COR). The wide variety of COR items that are represented in the anecdotes demonstrates the range of learning experiences that occur when teachers build on children's interests. Note, too, that these learning experiences involve not just the child whose actions were the original inspiration for a particular teaching strategy but also many other children in the group.

As Maria holds the teacher's "new baby," the teacher opens the baby present Maria painted and wrapped during work time.

Child Observations

INITIATIVE

TEACHER'S ANECDOTAL NOTES	*HIGH/SCOPE COR ITEM AND LEVEL*
At planning time Brianna said, "I'm going to take my Valentine cards and write my friends' names on the envelopes. Then I'll put them in their cubbies."	A. Expressing choices: (5) Child gives detailed description of intended actions.
At work time Megan laid a doll on top of a diaper and tried to pull the diaper up between the doll's legs. When this didn't work, she left the doll on the table and went to the sand table.	B. Solving problems: (2) Child identifies problems, but does not try to solve them, turning instead to another activity.
At large-group time Rachel sat and smiled while others sang and acted out a song about using various baby items.	C. Engaging in complex play: (2) Child shows interest in simple use of materials or simple participation in activities.
After Graham finished wrapping pretend baby-shower presents in the house area at work time, he returned the tape, markers, and remaining newspaper to the art area.	D. Cooperating in program routines: (4) Child participates in program routines without being asked.

SOCIAL RELATIONS

TEACHER'S ANECDOTAL NOTES	*HIGH/SCOPE COR ITEM AND LEVEL*
At outside time Madison invited Carol [a teacher] to come to the art fair and look at "the pretty pictures inside the boxes." She got two pocketbooks, gave one to Carol, and said, "Here's some money in case we buy something." This play continued for all of outside time with Madison enlisting another adult to play with her when the teacher had to "leave the fair."	E. Relating to adults: (4) Child sustains interactions with familiar adults.
For about half of work time, Audie played a game of trick or treat with Maria and James in which Maria passed out crumbled paper "treats" and James and Audie pretended to gobble them up.	F. Relating to other children: (4) Child sustains interactions with other children.
At work time, when Martin asked Brianna if she was making a Valentine card for him, Brianna replied, "Yes, because you're one of my friends."	G. Making friends with other children: (3) Child identifies a classmate as a friend.
"Don't say crazy to Natasha— it might hurt her feelings," said Steven to Julio, after Julio wondered aloud why Natasha was wearing a ballerina costume in February.	H. Engaging in social problem solving: (4) Child sometimes attempts to solve problems with other children independently, by negotiation or other socially acceptable means.
After Natasha pretended to flutter to the planning table, Kayla turned to her teacher and said, "She's very excited."	I. Understanding and expressing feelings: (5) Child responds appropriately to the feelings of others.

CREATIVE REPRESENTATION

TEACHER'S ANECDOTAL NOTES

HIGH/SCOPE COR ITEM AND LEVEL

At work time Saraya pressed Play-Doh into a muffin tin and said, "It's a cupcake for Graham's new baby."	J. Making and building: (4) Child uses materials to make a simple representation and says or demonstrates what it is.
At work time Julia got out the face-painting materials and a mirror. Then, as Kacey sat facing the mirror, Julia put three lines of paint on each of Kacey's cheeks and said, "There, now you look like a kitty."	K. Drawing and painting: (3) Child draws or paints simple representations.
At work time Maria stuffed pieces of paper inside a plastic pumpkin. Holding the pumpkin, she stood at the entrance to the house area and said, "I'm giving out the treats. Come over here."	L. Pretending: Child assumes the role of someone or something else, or talks in language appropriate to the assumed role.

MUSIC AND MOVEMENT

TEACHER'S ANECDOTAL NOTES

HIGH/SCOPE COR ITEM AND LEVEL

At outside time Olivia walked from one end of the play yard to the other holding a large broom. She said she was "cleaning up the mess."	M. Exhibiting body coordination: (4) Child moves around while manipulating an object.
At small-group time Jordan picked up straw pieces and pushed them into the modeling clay, using his thumb and his first two fingers.	N. Exhibiting manual coordination: (2) Child uses appropriate finger and hand motions to handle or pick up small objects.
At large-group time, as children sang and acted out a song about how baby items are used, Nathaniel made pushing movements with his hands to the words "push the stroller."	P. Following music and movement directions: (2) Child follows spoken instructions for a single movement.

LANGUAGE AND LITERACY

TEACHER'S ANECDOTAL NOTES

HIGH/SCOPE COR ITEM AND LEVEL

At greeting time when Adriana asked, "What means flutter?" Natasha demonstrated with her body, then turned and said, "**That** means flutter."	Q. Understanding speech: (3) Child responds to simple, direct, conversational sentences.
While cutting fruit for salad at small-group time, Graham said, "These blueberries make my fingers blue."	R. Speaking: (2) Child uses simple sentences of more than two words.

Continued on the next page.

Continued from the previous page.

TEACHER'S ANECDOTAL NOTES	HIGH/SCOPE COR ITEM AND LEVEL
At greeting time Leah asked Carol [a teacher] to read her the book **Scary, Scary Halloween.**	S. Showing interest in reading activities: (3) Child asks people to read stories or signs or notes.
At work time Megan went to the book area, got out the newspaper advertising supplements showing Valentine supplies, and sat on the couch looking through the supplements from front to back.	T. Demonstrating knowledge about books: (2) Child picks up books and holds them conventionally, looking at the pages and turning them.
At work time, as she and Megan looked at the newspaper advertising sections together, Frances said, "Look there's a **T.** That's in the store Target."	U. Beginning reading: (2) Child identifies some letters and numbers.
During small-group time Brianna drew a heart on a piece of construction paper and, inside it, wrote the message "I lve u." She said to Trey, who was sitting next to her, "I'm giving this to my Mom and it says **I love you.**"	V. Beginning writing: (4) Child writes some words or short phrases besides own name.

LOGIC AND MATHEMATICS

TEACHER'S ANECDOTAL NOTES	HIGH/SCOPE COR ITEM AND LEVEL
Steven took all the cut-in-half greeting cards out of the box and put them in two separate piles. Then he said, "These are from Christmas and these are the baby-shower ones."	W. Sorting: (4) In sorting, child groups objects together that are the same in some way and occasionally describes what has been done.
At small-group time, while cutting up fruit for salad, Graham said, "We had this fruit [points to blueberries] at our party, but not bananas."	X. Using the words *not, some,* and *all*: (4) Child uses the word *not* to identify the characteristic that excludes an object from a category.
At small-group time Yolanda put two bananas next to each other, pointed to them, and said, "Small, bigger."	Y. Arranging materials in graduated order: (2) Child arranges two or three items in graduated order, based on one characteristic such as size, shade of color, or texture.
As children gathered for large-group time around a pile of wrapped items, Nicole said, "Uh-oh, there are more children than presents."	AA. Comparing numbers of objects: (2) Child compares the quantities of small groups of objects, correctly using words like *more* and *less*.
At work time Brendan pointed to his favorite toys in the newspaper advertising supplement and said, "I want this, this, and this. That's three things."	BB. Counting objects: (3) Child correctly counts up to three objects.
At greeting time, while looking at the book **The New Baby,** Jack siad to Graham, "First your Mommy will have her baby and then mine is ntext."	DD. Describing sequence and time: (3) Child describes or represents a series of events in the correct sequence.

Adult Training Activities

This training experience is designed to enable participants to discuss the importance of celebrating special occasions with children in ways that are meaningful to them. Give participants the following directions:

Discuss the following two scenarios with your group members from the perspective of child choice, child creativity, and opportunities for problem solving.

Scenario One:

> *The adults in Preschool A carried out the following series of holiday activities. Three days before Thanksgiving, the adults conducted a small-group activity in which children had the choice of making a Pilgrim's hat or an Indian headband. The adults provided pre-cut materials for each project. Two days before the holiday all the children gathered at a long table decorated with a Thanksgiving tablecloth and a turkey center-piece, wearing the Pilgrim's hat or Indian headband they made the previous day. They ate their snack together while the adult explained the significance of the first Thanksgiving meal. The day before the holiday, children made Thanksgiving pictures to send home to parents. To help each child make a picture, the adult traced around the child's hand on a piece of white paper. Children were then asked to color in the finger outlines in different colors to make them look like turkey feathers. On the back of each picture the adult wrote "Happy Thanksgiving."*

Child Choice:

Child Creativity:

Opportunities for Problem Solving:

Scenario Two:

> *For several days before and after the Thanksgiving vacation, adults in Preschool B added the following materials to the classroom interest areas: suitcases, pie and muffin tins, real pumpkins and gourds, orange and brown construction paper and paint, grocery store circulars advertising the holiday food specials, cans and boxes of pumpkin-pie and bread mixes,*

books about turkeys and Thanksgiving stories, and orange Play-Doh.

Child Choice:

Child Creativity:

Opportunities for Problem Solving:

"Messy" 7 Materials

Pouring,

Filling,

Mixing, and

Molding

Every day for the first month of school, Kelly makes a plan to work at the sand and water table, which is now filled with sand. Even when she is last or nearly last to share her plans with the group, she still makes the same plan—she isn't influenced by hearing the other children's ideas. When Kelly reaches the sand-filled table, she plays quietly, using shovels, cups, funnels, and spoons as she fills plastic containers with sand, empties them, and fills them again. Sometimes, when filling a container, she stands on tiptoe and pours from high above the container; at other times she crouches, holding the container she is emptying close to the container she is filling.

In the beginning weeks of school Kelly rarely talks to classmates who are also playing at the table. When she does initiate an interaction, her usual approach is to fill up a plastic cup with sand and offer this "cup of coffee" to an adult or classmate. If the person pretends to sip it, she breaks into a chuckle and says, "It's poison."

It has been a particularly rainy October. One day at outside time Brendan is splashing in a mud puddle, jumping up and down laughing as he splashes. "Don't you think mud is wonderful?" he says. Inspired by Brendan's comment, the teaching team decides to add puddles of water to the sand and water table, which lately has been filled with sand. The next morning, children react in a variety of ways as they discover the puddles in the sand. As children approach the table, Jeania, another child, watches from a distance. Each time a new child begins to touch the wet sand, she says to the child, "That will make your clothes dirty—you'd better not." Brendan walks over to the table and immediately begins splashing the water with his hands. He explains to Victor, who is standing next to him, "I'm pretending my hands are my feet at outside time."

Soon a small group of children have gathered at the table, engrossed in sand play. Each child seems to experience the sand and water in a different way. Next to Brendan, Danna plunges her hands in the sand, chanting "Squishy, squishy, squishy" as the sand oozes through her fingers. Maria gets a shovel and digs a series of holes side by side, commenting that the water "is running from one hole into the next." As the children mix water with the dry sand, new play ideas emerge. Carleen, who always spends part of her summer holiday at a lake, bakes "mud pies" using round containers in various sizes. She makes each pie by filling a container with sand, patting down the top, flipping the container over on the sand, and carefully lifting it off. Then she inserts Popsicle sticks and twigs in the pie and sings "Happy Birthday." Adding to the party atmosphere at the sand table, Madison brings cookie-cutters and plates from the house area. She cuts out some sand "cookies" and arranges them on a plate. She explains that "it's almost holiday time" and the cookies are "to give to people who come to my house to visit."

◎

One December morning, Frances calls across the room to children gathered at the book area for greeting time. "Look," Frances shouts, "there's snow in the sand table." This causes a flurry of excitement—six children immediately leave the book area and gather around Frances. One of the adults stays with the remaining children in the book area and finishes the messages for the morning, which include an announcement about the snow surprise. Meanwhile, Barbara, the other adult, walks over to join the children at the snow-filled table. When she gets there Frances is explaining to children that "the blue bin with the mitten picture on the outside is the place where you get gloves to keep your hands warm." Barbara searches through the bin for a pair that will fit her hands, puts them on, leans down close to the children gathered around the table, and says, "I think my first plan will be to work right here." She begins digging in the snow with her hands as the children next to her pat the snow, dig in it, and plant pieces of plastic tubing upright in it.

For the rest of the week, while there is still snow to be had, Barbara and her team member refill the table daily with snow. As the days go by, children continue to poke, pat, and dig in the snow. One morning Audie is at the table making a tall mound of snow. He steps back from it, saying "Hey, a mountain. I want to go skiing," then leaves the table. He visits the toy and art areas and is back in a few minutes, bringing a small plastic person, tape, and two Popsicle sticks. He hands the materials to Barbara and says, "Here, hold the feet up while I put tape on the sticks." She does, and after he has attached the sticks to the toy person's feet he begins gliding his small skier up and down the snow mountain.

After watching Audie for a few minutes, Julia says, "I want to do that with a sled. Make me one, Audie." "Not now, I'm busy," he replies. James, who is also at the table, says to Julia, "I'll help you." After getting a toy person and a bottle cap to use as a sled, Julia unsuccessfully tries to fit the person inside the cap. When this doesn't work, she throws the cap and toy figure across the room and screams, "This doesn't work. I hate this game." Barbara moves closer to her, calmly making comments about how frustrating it is when something doesn't work the way you want it to. Julia climbs into Barbara's lap and continues to cry. Audie leans over Julia and suggests, "Try tape like I did." Julia then retrieves her materials from across the room, successfully applies Audie's suggestion, and pushes her sled down Audie's mountain for the rest of work time. As Audie and Julia continue with their runs down the mountain, James adds a row of plastic tubing alongside the mountain. He explains that these "pylons" are needed to mark the boundaries of the space for sledding and skiing, so that people "racing down the hill" won't crash into people walking below.

Exploring, Experimenting, and Representing With "Messy" Materials

The processes of filling, pouring, molding, mixing, and dumping are repeated over and over in young children's play. Children's interest in filling and emptying begins early in life. In home settings where infants, toddlers, and preschoolers are free to explore, it is common for adults to find the contents of shelves, cabinets, and boxes tossed across the floor. To a toddler, a container of crayons or felt markers is more likely to be seen as a toy for dumping and filling than as a collection of drawing tools.

Preschool-aged children are also fascinated with the motions and effects associated with filling and emptying. Like infants and toddlers, older preschoolers sometimes enjoy dumping containers of toys to make big piles. Sometimes they dump for the sake of dumping, finding satisfaction and comfort in the simple process of manipulating and controlling familiar materials. At other times they attach representational labels to their filling-and-emptying experiences. One morning shortly after Halloween, for example, Carleen and Donald took all the toys from the toy area shelf and piled them on the carpet. Using the toys to represent candy in a game of trick or treat, they enjoyed selecting pretend candy items from the pile.

Carleen and Donald's play is just one example of the many possible forms that filling-and-emptying play can take. When the materials for filling and emptying are expanded to include moldable materials such as snow, mud, and clay, the play possibilities also expand. Children use moldable materials in a variety of ways. Danna, when she squeezed the wet sand through her fingers, was interested in exploring the effects of a familiar, repetitive motion on a new material. Maria, on the other hand, was fascinated by the series of holes she had made in the wet sand and the effects she could create by manipulating this small environment. Still other children, like Carleen and Madison, used the same materials to represent personally important events and experiences.

Whatever their individual play interests, you can be sure that children will return again and again to the filling, emptying, and molding materials you provide. As you observe children playing with these materials, the High/Scope Child

Observation Record (COR) offers a helpful frame of reference for recording and interpreting the resulting learning experiences. Some of the observations teachers recorded about the play experiences described in the opening scenarios are highlighted in "Child Observations" on the next two pages. Next to each anecdotal note is a corresponding High/Scope COR item that the teachers used to identify an important dimension of the child's behavior.

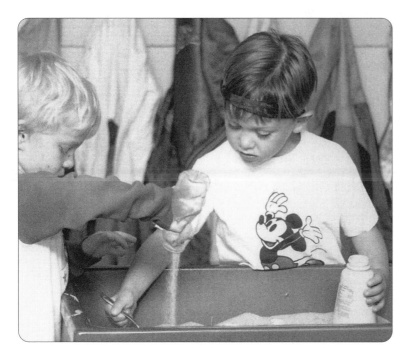

Filling and emptying can be a social experience. "I'll take a spoon of poison," says Mark to Brendan as they work at the sand and water table.

Supporting Children's Pouring, Filling, Mixing, Dumping, Molding

Our observations tell us that young children are natural dumpers and pourers, and that their fascination with filling and emptying continues even into the primary school years. We also know that young children usually find dumping and emptying easier than refilling or putting back, and this can create problems for adults worried about messes and disorder. With careful planning of your environment and thoughtful use of adult-child interaction strategies, however, you can support the child's need for dumping and pouring while keeping the messes created within manageable limits. Below are some of the ideas the teaching team generated for supporting the actions and interests of the children in the opening scenarios.

General Teaching and Interaction Strategies

✔ **Be aware that pouring, filling, and emptying are actions that often offer comfort and familiarity to young children.** Even though Kelly stayed at the sand-filled table repeating the same kinds of actions for almost every work time during the first weeks of school, teachers did not suggest that she play somewhere else. They were sensitive to her own timetable for exploring sand. Likewise, when she handed the "poison" cup of sand over and over again to adults, they never commented that she might want to do something else—instead, they entered Kelly's fantasy world and pretended to feel sick from sipping the poison. The teacher understood this as Kelly's way of initiating interactions with adults and other children and continued to support this behavior. Eventually Kelly began to initiate interactions in other ways.

Child Observations

INITIATIVE

TEACHER'S ANECDOTAL NOTES	*HIGH/SCOPE COR ITEM AND LEVEL*
At work time Audie announced that he wanted to "go skiing" as he played in a mountain of snow. He collected a plastic person, tape, and Popsicle sticks and asked Barbara [a teacher] to "hold the feet up while I put on the sticks."	B. Solving problems: (4) Child shows some persistence, trying several alternative methods to solve a problem.
At work time Kelly used shovels and containers to pour sand from one area of the sand and water table to another, sometimes pouring while standing tall, sometimes while crouching down low.	C. Engaging in complex play: (2) Child shows interest in simple use of materials or simple participation in activities.

SOCIAL RELATIONS

TEACHER'S ANECDOTAL NOTES	*HIGH/SCOPE COR ITEM AND LEVEL*
At outside time Brendan splashed in a puddle, then went up to Peter [a teacher] and said, "Don't you think mud is wonderful?"	E. Relating to adults: (3) Child initiates interactions with familiar adults.
At greeting time Frances was the first to discover snow in the sand and water table, and as children gathered around her to work she told them, "The blue bin with the mitten picture on the outside is the place where you get gloves to keep your hands warm."	F. Relating to other children: (3) Child initiates interactions with other children.
At work time when Julia requested Audie's help and was told that he was busy, James (who was also nearby) said, "I'll help you."	I. Understanding and expressing feelings: (3) Child shows awareness of the feelings of others.

CREATIVE REPRESENTATION

TEACHER'S ANECDOTAL NOTES	*HIGH/SCOPE COR ITEM AND LEVEL*
At work time Danna put her hands in the sand and water mixture and chanted, "Squishy, squishy, squishy" as it oozed through her fingers.	J. Making and building: (2) Child explores making-and-building materials.
At work time at the sand and water table Brendan splashed water with his hands and told Victor, "I'm pretending my hands are my feet at outside time."	J. Making and building: (4) Child uses materials to make a simple representation and says or demonstrates what it is.

Continued on the next page.

Continued from the previous page.

MUSIC AND MOVEMENT

TEACHER'S ANECDOTAL NOTES	HIGH/SCOPE COR ITEM AND LEVEL
At work time Carleen filled different-sized containers with sand, patting down and leveling off the sand in each container. She then turned the containers upside down and lifted the container away so the sand shape was left standing.	M. Exhibiting body coordination: (5) Child engages in complex movements.
With Barbara [a teacher] holding the Popsicle sticks in place, Audie taped them to the feet of a plastic person to make the skier he had described in his plan.	N. Exhibiting manual coordination: (4) Child manipulates small objects with precision.

LANGUAGE AND LITERACY

TEACHER'S ANECDOTAL NOTES	HIGH/SCOPE COR ITEM AND LEVEL
At work time, when she couldn't get her plastic person to stay in her bottle-cap sled, Julia threw the person and the bottle cap across the room. When Audie suggested, "Try tape" (as he had done to make a sled for his person), she retrieved the materials from across the room and used his idea to complete the task.	Q. Understanding speech: (3) Child responds to simple, direct, conversational sentences.
At work time Jeania told children who were touching wet sand, "That will make your clothes dirty . . . you'd better not."	R. Speaking: (2) Child uses simple sentences of more than two words.
At work time Julia watched Audie ski a toy person down the snow mountain. She said, "I want to do that with a sled."	R. Speaking: (3) Child uses sentences that include two or more separate ideas.

LOGIC AND MATHEMATICS

TEACHER'S ANECDOTAL NOTES	HIGH/SCOPE COR ITEM AND LEVEL
At work time Maria dug a series of holes in the sand and watched the water flow from hole to hole. She said the water was "running from one hole into the next."	CC. Describing spatial relations: (4) Child uses words that describe the direction of movement of things.
At work time James added plastic tubing to the side of the snow mountain, saying "It's so the people racing down the hill won't crash into other people."	CC. Describing spatial relations: (4) Child uses words that describe the direction of movement of things.
At work time, after making cookies out of wet sand, Madison explained that she made cookies because "It's almost holiday time." She said the cookies were "to give to people who come to my house to visit."	DD. Describing sequence and time: (5) When describing or representing a series of events in the correct sequence, child uses words for conventional time periods.

✔ **Use the actions and comments of the children as a source of teaching ideas.** When Brendan expressed his excitement about mud, teachers added water puddles to the sand-filled table, even though this meant cleanup times would have to be slightly longer and children's clothing would be messier. They also responded to Brendan's interest by introducing a song about mud (see strategy 3, "Large-Group Experiences," page 122).

Storing accessories for the sand and water table on a nearby shelf in separate bins enables children to start their work in an uncluttered space and, free of distractions, to choose the materials that best fit their plans. This also sets the stage for sorting experiences like this at cleanup time.

✔ **Be available to give children the help they may need in completing their plans, and be sensitive to the differing ways they may express their needs for help.** While playing at the snow-filled table, Audie and Julia requested Barbara's support for very different reasons and in very different ways. While Audie was able to make a straightforward request for the help he needed, Julia asked for help by crying and climbing into Barbara's lap. Yet Barbara was able to encourage both children to complete their plans because she listened carefully to each child, maintained a calm attitude, and responded sensitively to the children's feelings.

✔ **Help children break big tasks into smaller steps** so they can complete their plans as independently as possible. When Donald and Carleen began dumping toys in a big pile to represent Halloween candy, their teacher, Carol, helped them understand that cleaning up the toys would take a long time. She assisted them by giving them a cleanup warning several minutes earlier than usual and asking for their opinions about which items they would sort through as they began to put

Sometimes children get carried away with pouring and dumping, as when these children created a "fireworks explosion." When this happens the support of an understanding adult encourages children to take responsibility for returning the toys to their containers. The teacher's presence helps keep children engaged.

away the toys. Carol also stayed near them throughout the cleanup process and sorted alongside them, modeling playful ways of cleaning up to help keep them engaged in the task. For example, she built on the children's original trick-or-treat idea by pretending the various cleanup containers were trick-or-treat bags.

✔ **Store play accessories near, rather than in, the sand and water table.** Place containers, pouring and molding tools, and toy people and vehicles, for example, in plastic bins near the sand and water table. Children are more likely to develop and follow through on their own ideas when the play area itself is not crowded and cluttered with toys. Keeping a variety of extra play materials available nearby in easily accessible, well-organized containers will encourage children's inventiveness.

Indoor and Outdoor Materials to Add

Filling and emptying

1   If children, like Kelly, have been pretending to pour coffee with fill-and-empty materials, provide new and interesting smells and textures by filling the sand and water table with real coffee grounds. (To do this, save your used coffee grounds for several weeks. It won't be long until you have enough to fill the table.)

2   Put everyday objects that are not ordinarily used as containers near the sand and water table and watch children use them for filling and emptying. One teaching team tried this strategy with socks, mittens, and gloves; they found that children were fascinated by the changing shapes they could produce by filling the clothing items with sand.

3   To make improvised funnels for children to use in sand and water play, poke holes in the bottoms of paper, Styrofoam, or disposable plastic cups. Vary the size and number of the holes. The small plastic plant holders or pots that come with flats of bedding plants also work well for this purpose.

4   To provide opportunities for dumping and filling in another classroom area, put a set of different-sized clear plastic containers in your house area and fill them with small objects like dinosaur counters, poker chips, and Styrofoam packing bits. Add pots, pans, large slotted spoons, and ladles, and observe the ways children pour and mix the materials.

5   Add computer software programs such as *Kid Pix* (Broderbund Software) or *Dinosaurs Are Forever* (Merit Software) that enable children to fill and empty on the screen.

Working with water

6   If children have been exploring mud puddles outdoors and water puddles in the sand and water table indoors, make available materials that give children additional

opportunities to observe how water moves from place to place. Possible materials include water wheels, turkey basters, plastic squirting toys, hand-held egg beaters, and wire whisks. Observe which children use the materials in exploratory ways and which use them to represent everyday activities involving liquids.

7 To build on children's interest in mixing water with various materials, fill the sand and water table with one of these materials for mixing with the water: ice cubes, bubble bath, dishwashing soap, food coloring, or cooking oil. After about a week, try one of the other materials.

8 To provide a different kind of mixing experience with a different form of water, place icicles in paint containers to use as paintbrushes or as paint-mixing or blending tools.

9 In warm weather, support children's interest in mixing water with sand and soil by adding water sprinklers and hoses with nozzles near dirt or sand piles outdoors.

10 When your sand and water table is filled with water, place large buckets near the table. At cleanup time, encourage children to participate in a game of emptying the water from the table into the buckets and pouring it into the sink. On occasion reverse the process by encouraging children to fill the table when they make a plan to use water at work time.

Molding

11 If children have shown an interest in using snow, mud, or wet sand for molding, put materials near the sand and water table that offer different kinds of molding opportunities. Possible materials might include pails in a range of shapes and sizes, cookie-cutters, gelatin molds, and various kinds of shovels.

12 Make a wet sand pile outdoors. Near the pile make available larger shovels, digger trucks, and a collection of outdoor materials (acorns, leaves, tree bark).

13 In winter, bring snow shovels outdoors and help children build their own snow piles and mountain shapes. Encourage children to notice the imprints they make in the snow with their boots, shoes, or gloved hands.

14 To enable children to explore moldable forms of water, add snow, slush, or ice to the indoor environment, as teachers did in the play example. Also provide tools and containers outdoors that children can use for filling, emptying, molding, and exploring with the snow, slush, and ice. Have extra mittens on hand.

Because the teachers have added a small amount of water to the dry sand, these children have opportunities to use the sand for molding as well as for sifting and pouring.

Filling the table with snow enables children to try a new material for molding and to explore the properties of snow in a new setting.

Help children make connections between their indoor and outdoor play experiences by observing them closely and then following up on their ideas and interests. If children have been enjoying sledding outdoors, for example, provide appropriate materials so they can re-enact the experience indoors.

Planning And Recall Experiences

Filling and emptying

1 Fill a sock with sand and tie it securely. Ask children who are planning or recalling to toss it into the area of their work time plans or experiences and then to describe their ideas.

2 During cleanup time, make a single basket or bag available for all the children to fill with materials they used at work time. Ask each child to put something he or she used at work time in the bag. At recall time have each child pick a material from the bag, talk about how he or she used it, and place the material back on the shelf. Follow this process until the basket or bag is empty. The next day at planning time, get out the same bag or basket and have children fill it with items they plan to use at work time (one item per child). Children take turns picking out items and sharing their plans until the bag or basket is empty.

3 Provide a small cup of colored sand for each child at the table. One by one, children describe their work time plans or experiences while pouring their cup of sand into a larger bowl. Give children the choice of pouring from high or low positions (either standing on tiptoe to pour or crouching down low). After each child has taken a turn planning or recalling, have children take turns stirring the mixture.

Encourage children to notice and describe the changes created as the different colors mix together.

Working with water

4   Hold planning or recall time at the sand and water table, which you have already filled with water. Provide a pitcher and a water wheel and tell children you will be playing the game "Can you tell us your work time idea before the water wheel stops moving?" Children take turns sharing their plans or experiences as they pour the water from the pitcher into the water wheel. Children may share their ideas by speaking, pointing, or acting them out. When the wheel stops turning, the other children guess, comment, or ask questions about the ideas the child has shared. Be aware that some children may be so focused on pouring water and making the wheel go around that they will do this first before planning or recalling, or using the water wheel may simply become their plan.

5   Vary the previous strategy using different water-play materials. For example, bring empty containers marked with interest area symbols to the water-filled table. Ask children, one by one, to fill a turkey baster and squirt it into the container that stands for the area of their work time plans or experiences.

6   On another day gather around the empty sand and water table and ask children to take turns pouring a bucket of water into the table to fill it for work time. Each child shares his or her plans after pouring in a bucket of water.

Before starting his plan to work at the sand and water table, Christopher fills the table with buckets of water from a nearby sink, maneuvering the heavy bucket without help.

Molding

7 Build on children's interest in making cakes and cookies out of wet sand by making a set of sand cookies using cookie-cutters of various shapes. Place a different-shaped sand cookie on a plate for each child, and put the cookie-cutters used inside a paper bag. One person then reaches in to pick out the cookie-cutters one by one. When a cookie-cutter is selected, the child with the matching cookie describes his or her plans or experiences.

8 Draw the area symbols on Popsicle sticks and stand them upright in a giant sand cake. As individual children describe their plans or experiences they choose a "candle" from the cake to represent an area they plan to work in or have worked in.

9 Re-create a pretend scene from a child's molding experiences and use this as a starting point for the children's planning or recalling. For example, in Audie and Julia's class children gathered around the snow table for planning and recall times and helped the teacher re-create Audie's skier, Julia's sledder, and the snow mountain. As individual children took their turns planning or recalling, they first slid one of the toy figures down the snow mountain and then related their plans or experiences.

Small-Group Experiences

Filling and emptying

1 If children, like Kelly, have been using the same materials over and over again for filling and emptying, provide new materials for filling and emptying and watch to see how children use them. Inspired by Kelly's repetitive play with sand, the teachers planned a small-group experience in which each child was given a collection of small toys: teddy bear counters, large plastic pegs, bottle caps, and poker chips. On the table they also placed an assortment of plastic containers and plates of varying sizes and shapes. The teachers observed as some children used the materials for filling and emptying and others for pretending.

2 If you have filled your sand and water table with an unusual material, such as coffee grounds, plan a small-group experience around the removal of this material. Have children gather around the table filled with coffee grounds (or other material). Give children containers or digging tools (buckets, shovels, spoons, and so forth) and explain that it is time to remove the old material and refill the table with something else. Enlist everyone's help.

Working with water

3 Gather around a large plastic swimming pool filled with water or dry sand. Make a variety of containers available (enough so there are several for each child) so that each child has opportunities to pour from one container to another. Observe to see which children use the materials in a solitary way and which children pour, fill,

and empty while carrying on conversations with others; consider your observations in terms of children's developing social and language abilities.

4 To provide tactile exploration experiences for children, mix a batch of Plaster of Paris, following the directions on the box, and give each child a portion in a personal container. Also provide materials that children can use for imprinting, such as paper clips, corks, and bottle caps. Observe to see how children use the materials and whether they also try to make impressions of their body parts in the plaster.

Molding

5 If children have shown interest in molding with wet sand, mud, or other materials, offer them home-made "Silly Putty" for a different kind of molding experience. To make a smooth-textured, shiny putty, mix together equal parts of white glue and liquid starch.

6 After children have had snow-molding experiences at the sand and water table, take them outside to make a large outdoor version of a child's indoor snow creation. In Audie's classroom the teacher suggested that the children make a big snow mountain outside like Audie's. The teacher provided tools and materials children could use for patting, digging, and poking in the snow: tree branches, snow shovels, soup ladles, plastic measuring cups, and different-sized hairbrushes.

Large-Group Experiences

Filling and emptying

1 Obtain one chair per child and arrange the chairs all over the large-group meeting space. Explain to children that you will be playing a music tape for a game of "fill and empty the chairs." As the music plays, children dance around and between the chairs. When the music stops, children "fill up the chairs" by finding one to sit on. When the music starts again, they "empty the chairs" by standing up and moving around them. ("Bossa Nova" from Volume 7 of the *Rhythmically Moving* recording series, High/Scope Press, works well with this activity.)

Working with water

2 This strategy is intended to be used at the beginning of large-group time as a transition from the previous activity. Children can join in the activity as they join the group. Begin the activity by inviting children to imitate a child's actions they have observed at the sand table. For example, "Let's pretend to be Kelly at the sand table pouring her poison coffee from way up high. . . . Now let's pretend to be Kelly pouring the coffee from way down low." Ask children for their own ideas about what to pretend to pour or mix next, and from what position.

3 If you have observed children squeezing wet sand or mud through their fingers at work time or outside side, re-enact this experience with the group. Open the activity (and provide a signal for children to begin gathering for large-group time) by chanting "Squishy, squishy, squishy" as you manipulate your hands and fingers in imitation of children's actions. Ask children to suggest other words to describe what moving their fingers in wet sand or mud might feel like and to chant those words. Then chant or sing the song "I Love Mud" (by Rick Charette, from *Two for the Show*, a cassette recording by the Song Sisters) as follows:

> Mud, mud, I love mud.
> I'm absolutely, positively, wild about mud.
> You can't go around it.
> You have to go through it.
> Beautiful, fabulous, super-duper mud.

Observe the many creative ways children combine molding materials with other materials to carry out their plans. Here Kacey is making a "blueberry pie" to go along with the "coffee" she is serving Maria.

Molding

4 Build a pretending game around creations you have observed children making out of sand, snow, or mud during previous activities. Have children move as if they were molded in various shapes, including the shapes of children's creations. Encourage children to share other ideas on ways they could mold their bodies. For example, after Audie made a snow mountain at school, teachers asked children to act out the ways their bodies might look if molded into the shape of Audie's mountain. They also asked children to assume the shape of a big hill near the school.

What We Learned From Our Observations of Children

After teachers tried the strategies suggested in this chapter, they observed children's activities to see what kinds of learning experiences were occurring. They observed that children's work with messy materials encouraged learning and development in all ability areas. The selection of anecdotes presented in "Child Observations" on the next two pages documents some of these learning experiences. The anecdotes are classified according to the High/Scope key experience categories.

Child Observations

CREATIVE REPRESENTATION

At large-group time Brianna made the shape of a mountain with her body, then suggested the next shape for the group to try: "a dog that's happy because Mommy came home."

At work time Daniel brought the small, colored, wooden blocks to the snow-filled table, stacked them up as if they were bricks, and called his structure an "igloo."

During greeting time on the first morning the sand and water table was filled with coffee grounds, Kelly said, "Hey, it smells like coffee in here."

LANGUAGE AND LITERACY

*At outside time Christopher took a pile of acorns and arranged them in the snow to make a **C** and an **H.** When his dad came to pick him up he said, "Look what I did."*

As Carleen was pouring sand into the swimming pool at small-group time, she leaned closer to Barbara [a teacher] and said, "This sand is like the time my Mommy took me to the beach. . . . We have a cottage at the lake, you know."

At large-group time, the group was making up verses to the "I Love Mud" song. When the group was asked how it might feel to move their fingers in mud, Jeania suggested the verse "Dirty, dirty, dirty."

INITIATIVE AND SOCIAL RELATIONS

At recall time as children were imitating one another's activities at the sand and water table, Patrick suggested that the group act out the motions of stirring "around and around" like a cement truck.

At work time, Saraya squirted water on her clothing with the turkey baster. She then went to her cubbie, got a dry shirt, and changed her clothing without the help of a teacher.

MOVEMENT

While at the coffee-filled table at work time, Tiffany explained how to make a pile of coffee grounds: "First you scoop, then you tap it."

At work time, Michael hopped from foot to foot as he squirted water from the turkey baster. He continued to hop on alternate feet until the baster was empty.

As she painted with an icicle at large-group time, Megan said to Frances, "Look what happens when I move it around—it drips down my picture."

MUSIC

During a large-group time game of "fill and empty the chairs" Carleen moved to the music by pretending to skate around and between the chairs. When the music stopped she sat in the chair closest to her.

While swinging on the tire swing at outside time Julia sang the song "Mud" over and over.

Continued on the next page.

Continued from the previous page.

Describing his experience of squirting water from the turkey baster at work time, Michael told children in his recall group that the water made a "plopping" sound; he then imitated the sound.

CLASSIFICATION

At planning time Elyse said, "I'm going to use the mittens in the sand table instead of the buckets "cause they're soft."

Brendan spent all of outside time experimenting with the hose nozzle, changing the water flow from a fine mist to a steady stream.

SERIATION

"Look," said Frances as she filled a glove with sand at work time, "the fingers are getting bigger."

Kelly remained at the sand-filled table after planning and arranged the area symbol signs according to their height. [The area symbols were attached to Popsicle sticks to make small signs, which were standing upright in the sand.] She explained as she pointed to the signs that they were "small, big, taller."

At planning time Audie said, "My skier will go down the mountain the fastest of everybody. Watch." He then used a fast motion to push his skier down the slope.

NUMBER

At recall time Madison looked inside Kelly's basket and said, "Ooh, that's more than one. The teacher said bring one."

At planning time Elyse said she was going to the sand table to use the flower pots "with the many holes."

At planning time, after four children had poured and mixed their colored sand while describing their plans, Corey said, "So that's what happens after four cups mix colors. It's pretty."

SPACE

During work time, while looking through the photo album of children's activities at preschool, Randi said, "That's the day we made the snow mountain outside, over there by the tree."

When using a sock filled with sand as a planning prop, Audie said, "I'm going to throw it far away into the computer area."

TIME

At planning Maria told the other children "The water has something new, not like yesterday with the bubbles."

When working with plaster of Paris at small-group time Jeff said, "I used this before. It's going to get hard."

*When large-group time was over, Alex lay on the floor and said, "I never get a turn, not tomorrow, not yesterday, **never.**"*

Adult Training Activities

This training activity is designed to help adults see that the anecdotes they record about children's actions, language, and experiences can fit more than one of the items on the High/Scope Child Observation Record (COR). For this activity, participants use the anecdotes and matching COR items and levels given in "Child Observations," page 113, as well as the list of additional COR items and levels provided here.

1. Ask participants, working in small groups, to look at the selection of anecdotes and to discuss how each one reflects the High/Scope Child Observation Record item and level that are matched to it.

2. Pass out the list of additional COR items and ask participants to discuss how each of the original anecdotes might also be matched to an item or items on this list. In the discussion that follows highlight the idea that most play incidents involve more than one aspect of child development.

Additional High/Scope COR Items and Levels

A. Expressing choices: (2) Child indicates a desired activity or place of activity by saying a word, pointing, or some other action.

B. Solving problems: (3) Child uses one method to try to solve a problem, but if unsuccessful, gives up after one or two tries.

E. Relating to adults: (4) Child sustains interactions with familiar adults.

F. Relating to other children: (3) Child initiates interactions with other children.

H. Engaging in social problem solving: (4) Child sometimes attempts to solve problems with other children independently, by negotiation or other socially acceptable means.

J. Making and building: (2) Child explores making-and-building materials.

J. Making and building: (3) Child uses materials to make something but does not say whether it is meant to represent something else.

L. Pretending: (2) Child uses one object to stand for another or uses actions or sounds to pretend.

R. Speaking: (4) Child uses sentences that include two or more ideas with descriptive details.

Food-Related Play 8

Cooking,

Eating, and

Pretending

I t is the day after a field trip to a local pizza shop, during which children observed and participated in pizza-making. The teachers have added pizza-making materials to the house area for children to use independently at work time, if this is their work time choice. The materials include pre-sliced English muffins; bowls filled with real tomato sauce, grated cheese, sliced mushrooms, and pepperoni slices; large cookie sheets. A message about the addition of these materials is posted on the message board and was discussed at greeting time.

Kayla and Jordan, who have both made plans to make pizza, are the first to arrive at the table in the house area. Kayla immediately takes charge: "I'm going to put the muffins on the tray. Jordan, you get the spoon and put tomato sauce on top of each one." After neatly arranging the muffins in even rows on a baking sheet, Jordan begins spooning sauce on top of each one. "Whoa," says Kayla to Jordan, "there's too much on this one and not enough over here." Jordan continues his work, disregarding Kayla's warnings. Soon there is tomato sauce on the tray between all the rows of muffins. Then Kayla calls out to her teacher, Ann, who is standing nearby, "I'm frustrated with Jordan. He won't listen to my words and he's making a big mess with the sauce."

Meanwhile another child, Madison, enters the area, takes the spoon out of Jordan's hand, and says, "Here, let me show you." She gets an unused muffin and proceeds to scoop a spoonful of sauce on it. As she does, this she explains, "This is how to cook, Jordan. First, take a spoon with sauce and put it on the top. Then, use the back of the spoon to spread it all around to the edges." As she hands the spoon *back to Jordan she says, "Now you try it." Kayla and Ann watch Jordan as he imitates Madison's actions. (Later, Madison's mom explains that Madison often helps with cooking at home.) Ann asks Kayla if she is still feeling frustrated, and she replies, "Only about the mess in between." Ann answers, "So it bothers you that there is sauce in between the muffins?" "Yes," says Kayla, "I'd better start over." She takes the muffins off the tray, sets them aside, and takes the tray to the sink where she washes off the extra tomato sauce. When she returns, she works together with Jordan and Madison to complete the tray of pizzas. Madison suggests to Jordan that he spoon the sauce on the pizzas, after which she will sprinkle on the cheese. Kayla begins putting mushrooms and pepperoni on the pizzas, but is interrupted by Madison, who points to the picture of a muffin pizza on the recipe card, saying "Follow the recipe or it will taste funny." Then Kayla begins putting two mushroom pieces and one pepperoni slice on each pizza, as shown on the card.*

It is lunch time at a full-day child care program. One by one, children leave the large-group meeting space, go to the bathroom for toileting and hand-washing, and retrieve their lunch boxes on the way to the table. As children sit at the tables and begin opening up their lunches, their teacher, Stephanie, hears Tanuka ask David what his note for the day says. (His mother always includes a note with his lunch.) He unfolds the paper and says, "I think it says 'Have a great day.'" Meanwhile, Diana complains to Stephanie, "Cottage cheese again! I had that yesterday, too, and I'm sick of the way it tastes." Before Stephanie can respond, Sue says she loves cottage cheese and offers to trade some of her own peanut butter sandwich for Diana's cottage cheese. Michael is at the microwave. He says he is waiting for the microwave to beep, so he can push the "white rectangle" button to open the microwave door. When his spaghetti is done, he asks Stephanie to put it back in the oven so he can have his lunch "warmer still." Children continue to talk for a few more minutes as they unwrap food, negotiate food trades, and help one another open their juice boxes. Then quiet settles over the room as children begin eating.

A few minutes later a conversation begins. "Where does peanut butter come from and why is this bread like a heart?" says Diana, who is smiling as she eats part of Sue's sandwich. "From the store, silly," answers Sue, "and my Daddy cut the bread with a cookie-cutter like the one by the Play-Doh." "Why do you eat with sticks?" David asks Min, who responds by saying "Because I'm Chinese, except last night we went to McDonald's at the drive-through and I ate my food with my fingers." David replies, "I go to McDonald's, too, but on the inside where they have the place to climb and jump." The sound of children's conversation is soon replaced by a commotion; children are noisily sorting through the leftover paper and food and deciding what goes in the trash, what goes in the recycling bins, and what gets wrapped and saved in the lunch boxes. Taryn suddenly knocks over her juice cup (the only spill of this lunch day), and while she gets a sponge to clean up the juice, Tanuka offers to put the rest of Taryn's lunch items in their proper places.

"Come here, it's time to eat now," 3-year-old Elyse shouts at Malinda, her teacher, from the house area where she has been busily stirring a mixture of teddy bear counters, poker chips, and plastic star shapes in a large saucepan. As Malinda walks over, Elyse begins spooning the mixture onto plates, using a big ladle. Malinda sits down and Elyse says, "Okay, you be Greg [Elyse's father's name] and I'll be the mommy." Then Elyse says to Malinda, "Do you want to eat your eggs now?" Malinda answers, "I'd love to, because I'm hungry and they smell so good." Malinda then picks up a plastic star and pretends to put it to her mouth. "No," yells Elyse, "you have to use this." She hands Malinda a fork with several plastic stars on it and Malinda pretends to use the fork to eat the eggs. "Thank you," says Malinda, "these are tasty eggs." Elyse picks up the large saucepan, leaving Malinda alone at the table, and takes it to the block area where several children are pretending to "drive in a Batmobile car." She leans over the children in the "car" and says, "Do you want eggs?" After repeating her question six times and getting no response from the Batmobile-riders, she sets the pan down on the block area floor and joins children in the art area who are playing with silly putty.

Food for Thought: Growing Bodies and Growing Minds

As these examples illustrate, food is central in the lives of young children. Starting at a very early age, children communicate food preferences frequently and adamantly. Children also display a wide range of approaches to eating, as the above scenarios demonstrate. Any adult who regularly shares meals with children deals with children who complain habitually about the snack or lunch selection of the day, children who seem happy eating practically anything, children who are so concerned about staying neat and dry that they wipe their mouths with napkins after each bite of food, and children who show no sign of discomfort if the spaghetti they're eating gets all over their hands and face.

Like other parts of the daily routine, meal and snack times are educational times. This child is sorting out uncooked kernels as he eats popcorn.

Child choice and "learning by doing" are central concepts in the High/Scope approach. Since food is of definite interest to children and since its preparation and consumption provide many opportunities for active learning, we recommend that adults view food-related experiences as educational activities. Thus, regular planning, careful child observation, and thoughtful interaction with children are just as important for mealtimes and snacks as they are for other parts of the daily routine. Keeping this in mind, teachers recorded the anecdotal notes presented in "Child Observations" on pages 132–133 as they observed the experiences of children that open this chapter. They then interpreted the observations in terms of the High/Scope key experiences, grouping the anecdotes according to the High/Scope key experience categories.

Supporting Children's Food-Related Experiences

Caring adults concerned about the health and well-being of children often worry about the kinds of food children request, the amounts they eat, and the ways they consume it. Their concern for children's health and hygiene often leads them to use food as a reward ("If you eat all the green beans, I'll give you an ice cream cone for dessert") or punishment ("You had an accident in your pants today so you can't have any candy tonight"). Adults are also influenced by their own childhood experiences and by the expectations of others as they deal with such issues as table manners, food waste, and young children's tendency to explore and experiment with food.

Peeling your own bananas or pouring your own juice makes snack an active learning experience.

Deciding if, when, and how to set limits on children's food-related behaviors is especially difficult for teaching teams because of team members' varied personal beliefs about food and their concerns about children's nutrition. Such decisions are even more difficult to make in full-day programs where more meals are eaten and children bring lunches from home. Issues such as whether children should be permitted to trade foods from their lunches can be difficult to resolve. However, as with any other interest of children, the approach adults take to children's food-related experiences can influence the learning that occurs during such experiences. Therefore it is important for the teaching team to discuss these issues thoughtfully and to consider them within a developmental framework.

Listed next are teaching ideas developed specifically for the children in the examples that open this chapter. These strategies and experiences help to create an environment where children's interest in cooking, eating, and pretending about food is encouraged and supported.

General Teaching and Interaction Strategies

✔ **When you hear children ask questions such as "Where does peanut butter come from?" respond to their curiosity by planning field trips and other active group experiences that help children learn firsthand about the origins of food.** Plan to take children to places where food grows, is purchased, or is prepared by others, and plan small-group experiences that help children understand the origins of foods. Diana's question about peanut butter led the teaching team to plan a field trip to the grocery store and a small-group activity in which they used a food processor to make peanut butter from whole shelled peanuts.

✔ **Provide real tools for children to use when they are cooking or pretending to cook and eat together.** In the first scenario, the adults provided baking sheets,

A field trip to a place where food really grows gives children a better understanding of food origins .

large spoons, bowls, and real food items that were similar to those the children had seen adults using at home. This gave Madison and the other children the chance to imitate the actions of important adults in their lives. Also, it is far less frustrating for children to stir, pour, and serve using big saucepans, ladles, and adult-sized plates than when using doll-sized tea sets and utensils.

✔ **Always consider safety issues when preparing food with children.** Michael's interest in the microwave is supported when adults found a safe way he could participate—the teacher encouraged Michael to wait for the beeping sound and then push the button that makes the microwave door pop open. It's also important to model and encourage health habits such as washing hands before handling food and brushing teeth after eating.

✔ **When preparing foods with children, plan on having extra ingredients available.** As with any other skill that children are acquiring, food handling requires practice. In addition, preschoolers usually need to explore materials before they can use them for a purpose. Therefore, don't be surprised or alarmed if children waste some of the ingredients, particularly if they are new to food preparation. Expect that juice will spill, muffins will slip out of children's hands and fall on the floor, berries and raisins will disappear before being added to the batter, and some of the finished product will be eaten before it reaches the table.

When involving children in food preparation activities, take special safety precautions, as this teacher does by staying close by and designating a spot for the child's free hand.

Child Observations

CREATIVE REPRESENTATION

At work time Elyse called Malinda [a teacher] to the house area and told her she should "be Greg." Elyse announced, "I'm the mommy" and began spooning a mixture of teddy bear counters, poker chips, and plastic stars (which she called "eggs") onto a plate for "Greg" to eat.

LANGUAGE AND LITERACY

At lunch David unfolded his note for the day and told Tanuka, "I think it says 'Have a great day.'"

Madison showed Kayla the picture on the pizza recipe card (which showed two mushroom slices and one pepperoni piece on each English muffin) after she observed Kayla putting more of these toppings on both of the pizzas she was making.

INITIATIVE AND SOCIAL RELATIONS

At work time, while making English muffin pizzas, Kayla told Ann [a teacher], "I'm frustrated with Jordan. He won't listen to my words and he's making a big mess with the sauce." Then she took the muffins off the cookie tray, went to the sink, washed the tomato sauce off the tray, and put the muffins back on the clean tray. She told Ann that there had been "mess in between."

While Taryn was cleaning up her milk spill at lunch time, Tanuka offered to put away the rest of Taryn's lunch items.

MOVEMENT

When making English muffin pizzas at work time Madison told Jordan, "This is how to cook, Jordan. First, take a spoon with sauce and put it on top. Then, use the back of the spoon to spread it all around the edges."

MUSIC

After the microwave beeped four times, Michael pushed the white button to open the door.

✔ **Encourage children to take responsibility for their own actions by having cleanup materials readily available.** Sponges located at the children's level enabled Taryn to clean her own spill. You might also set out whiskbrooms, dustpans, and, if possible, a handheld sweeper.

✔ **Set a specific time aside each week during which actual food preparation, like the pizza-making experience described above, is planned.** In that particular setting every Wednesday was cooking day; for every Wednesday's work time, staff set out the materials for simple snacks such as fruit and vegetable salads, tortillas with grated cheese, hummus sandwiches on pita bread, Jell-O, yogurt mixed with fresh or frozen fruits, frozen pancakes and waffles, peanut butter and celery stalks. Since the adults were careful to offer materials that children could use indepen-

CLASSIFICATION

Tanuka held up a plastic bag left from Taryn's lunch and said to Stephanie [an adult], "This is to recycle, right?"

At lunch Min told David that even though she eats with chopsticks "because I'm Chinese," she also eats food with her fingers when going through the "drive-through" at McDonald's.

SERIATION

At lunch Michael asked Stephanie [a teacher] to put his lunch in the microwave for a little longer so that his food would get "warmer still."

NUMBER

After Madison showed her the pizza picture on the recipe card, Kayla put two mushroom slices and one piece of pepperoni on each English muffin as shown on the picture.

SPACE

Elyse filled the saucepan with an assortment of materials she called "eggs," then emptied the contents of the pan onto several plates.

David told Min at lunch, "I go to McDonald's, too, but on the inside where they have the place to climb and jump."

TIME

At work time Elyse asked Malinda, "Do you want to eat your eggs now?"

At lunch Diana told Stephanie, "Cottage cheese again! I had that yesterday."

dently, adults could circulate freely throughout the center as they always did at work time. Food preparation experiences might also be planned for small-group time. Such activities need not be provided on the same day each week, but when they are, the children have an opportunity to learn about the days of the week in a way that makes sense to them and to look forward to and prepare for a particular kind of experience.

✔ **When problems arise as children prepare foods, let children work things out on their own as much as possible.** When Kayla complained to Ann, her teacher, that Jordan was getting too much sauce on the pizza tray, Ann avoided getting involved immediately. By pausing, she gave Madison the chance to show Jordan a different way to put sauce on muffins. This play expanded as the children decided together

To reduce waiting periods during cooking experiences, make sure you have enough materials for each child. In this small-group experience each child cracks his or her own egg to scramble in a personal bowl.

what pizza toppings to use, who should add them, and how many pieces of each topping should go on each pizza.

Indoor and Outdoor Materials to Add

Cooking

1 If children have shown an interest in food preparation, add cookbooks and a recipe box to the book and house area. Add magazines featuring food to the book and art areas so children can express their individual food preferences in their reading and art activities.

2 Select tools for cooking that complement specific food preparation activities of interest to children. If you are planning to set out real ingredients for a food activity at work time or small-group time, also set out the appropriate tools: cheese graters for taco-making, potato-scrapers for potato peeling, pancake flippers for making pancakes, plastic bowls for mixing. After the tools have been used for the specific cooking activity, add them permanently to the house area to encourage pretend cooking. To further encourage imaginary cooking, supplement the actual cooking utensils with empty food cartons and boxes (cake-mix boxes, egg cartons).

3 Put props in your dress-up area that cooks might use at home or in restaurants—a chef's hat, aprons, a wok, hot mitts, and so forth.

4 To build on children's interest in where food comes from, set up a grocery store area in your house or block area. Include a cash register, different-sized paper and plastic bags, unopened canned goods, empty cereal boxes, egg cartons, and empty plastic peanut butter jars.

Eating

5 To support related role play after visiting restaurants on field trips bring back menus and other props (for example, empty pizza boxes) and add them to the house area. Ask parents to request menus from food establishments they visit with their children.

6 Some classrooms choose to set up a space for eating as a choice available every day during work time and as a replacement for a scheduled snack time. Providing simple foods and serving materials (for example, a pitcher of juice, crackers, cups) will create an opportunity for adults to observe the ways children help themselves to the foods and the kinds of conversations they have while sharing food together.

7 To build on children's interest in food preferences, add related books to the book area (for example, *Green Eggs and Ham* by Dr. Seuss, *Lunch* by Denise Fleming, *The Rinky-dink Cafe* by Maggie S. Davis, and *Dinner at the Panda Palace* by Stephanie Calmenson).

8   Add tablecloths, place mats, napkins, napkin rings, and other materials for serving and displaying food to the house area. Build on children's experiences with special-occasion meals by providing accessories: one classroom added vases and artificial flowers for flower arranging and a pair of candlestick holders with an assortment of candles.

Planning and Recall Experiences

Cooking

1   Following a class trip to a pizza parlor, take an empty pizza box and draw a large, pizza-sized circle inside the box. To represent the interest areas in your classroom, divide the pizza drawing into "slices," one slice for each interest area in your classroom. Attach an interest area symbol, photo, or object from the area to each slice. To give children practice in using a new cooking implement, give the child who is sharing plans or experiences a pizza cutter. Ask the child to cut on or near the outline of the slice representing his or her chosen interest area.

2   Bring to the planning/recall table a prop related to a child's specific cooking interest (hot mitt, spatula, pizza cutter, chef's hat made out of a paper bag with a crumpled top). The child whose turn it is to plan or recall wears or holds the prop while sharing work time ideas.

3   If children, like Madison, have been using a large bowl or saucepan for pretend cooking, use the same item as a prop during recall time. Put into the bowl or pan materials you saw children using at work time. Provide a fork or ladle and ask the children, one at a time, to scoop out the materials they used during work time and then to recall what they did.

To encourage food-related pretend play in your house area, choose plastic food that represents the foods you see children enjoying at snack and lunch.

4   Bring to the planning table cooking tools related to a real or pretend cooking activity you observed during a previous work time or small-group time. Ask children to go to the interest area they plan to work in (or worked in) and bring back a material they plan to use (or did use). As individual children share their plans or experiences, they use the utensils you've brought to the

table to "mix in" their ideas. Then "serve" the food you've made. If you are enacting wok-cooking, for example, set a large wok on the table and give each child chopsticks. Individual children show the group their chosen item, then "stir-fry" the item in the wok. After all plans or experiences have been shared, pretend to serve the stir-fried dish and have children use the chopsticks to eat it.

Eating

5 To simulate the conversation-stimulating effect of a meal, cover the planning/recall table with a tablecloth and place three lunch boxes on it. Ask three children at a time to put something in a lunch box they plan to use (or did use) at work time. Use the items each child brings back to the table as a starting point for conversation as you talk with individual children about their work time plans or experiences.

6 To support children's curiosity about different foods and their interest in sharing food, pass a tray of different kinds of crackers around the planning/recall table. When a child has finished eating, have that child plan or recall.

7 To build on the experiences of a child in your classroom who, like David, receives notes in his lunch box, draw interest area symbols on small pieces of paper, fold them up, and place them in a lunch box on the planning/recall table. Ask each child who is planning or recalling to pick a note and to pretend to be the child who receives lunch-box notes. The child reads the area symbol on the note selected, and then discusses whether his or her own plans or experiences include that area. You might also ask children to write and read their own notes about their plans or experiences. (Accept all forms of writing, including scribbles, letters, symbols, and words, as well as children's unique ways of reading.)

8 Ask children to pretend they are customers and wait-persons at a restaurant. As one child at a time shares work time plans or experiences, another child uses a pad of paper and a pencil to "write down" the ideas of the child who is planning or recalling.

9 Set up a booth to sit behind and ask children to pretend it is the drive-through window at a fast-food restaurant. Have children line up their "cars" next to the window and pretend they are waiting to give their orders. As each child reaches the window, give him or her a steering-wheel prop. Then ask the child to tell his or her work time plans or experiences to the person sitting behind the booth.

Small-Group Experiences

Cooking

1 If children have been enacting or talking about sandwich-making, plan a series of small-group activities using bread, cookie-cutters in a variety of shapes, and various sandwich spreads or fillings. Give children the bread and cookie-cutters first, and

after children have cut the bread into cookie-cutter shapes give them the fillings to put on top of or between the bread slices. Some possible fillings to be provided on different days include mustard and cheese; peanut butter and jelly; hummus; cream cheese and cucumbers; tofu slices, mustard, and sprouts.

2 To help children experience some new ways of using a familiar food, make peanut butter balls with children. Provide peanut butter, nonfat milk, honey, and sesame seeds. Don't worry about proportions; instead encourage children to focus on the changes that take place when ingredients are combined. At another small-group time, make the same snack with children using a recipe.

3 Make bird treats with children by dipping or rolling pine cones in peanut butter and birdseed.

4 Provide ingredients that children can explore and experiment with to make simple snacks. With the ingredients offer the utensils needed for mashing, chopping, or spreading: for example, spoons, blunt knives, forks, or spatulas. Each of the following could be used for one small-group time:

- Cooked squash and cooked rice for children to scoop and mix together.
- Parmesan cheese in a shaker box and cooked macaroni.
- Cooked pasta tubes and cottage cheese and cooked spinach for stuffing the tubes.
- Hard-boiled eggs to peel and mash; mayonnaise.

Eating

5 Build on a child's unique eating customs by providing similar tools or materials for all the children. To follow up on David's interest in Min's use of chopsticks, the teaching team provided a pair of chopsticks for each child and a collection of small objects and bowls. They watched as children experimented with using the chopsticks to pick up or move the objects.

6 If children have been discussing their food preferences, provide another way for them to express these preferences by offering magazines featuring a variety of foods. Page through the magazines with children, and encourage them to look for and talk about the foods they like and dislike. Provide scissors, paper, and glue for those children who want to cut out pictures to make a food collage.

7 If children have been discussing or re-enacting their experiences at fast-food restaurants, take your group on a field trip to a local fast-food restaurant. Ask the workers to donate a variety of props (cups with lids, straws, napkins, cardboard food boxes, ketchup and mustard packets, and paper place mats). The next day, hold small-group time in the house area. Encourage children to use the donated props in addition to the materials already in the area.

8 If children have shown interest in eating tubular pasta or o-shaped cereals, provide a different kind of experience with these foods. Set out pipe cleaners, pieces

of string with masking tape on one end, and some of the pasta (in dry form), or cereal. Watch as children make various creations with the materials, and don't be surprised if children eat their food creations.

9 Arrange to tour the kitchen and dishwashing area of a local restaurant with your small group. When you return to school, give children aprons, sponges, plastic dishes, and silverware and gather around a sand and water table filled with water. Encourage the children to pretend they are washing the dishes at the restaurant.

10 Prepare a basket of teddy bear counters and inch-cube blocks for each child. Before passing out the baskets, tell a short story about a teddy bear family that went to a restaurant for dinner. As you tell the story, enact it using your own set of materials. Then pass out the children's materials and watch to see which of them role-play a dinner meal with the materials.

Large-Group Experiences

Cooking

1 Make up a song about the day's cooking experiences to a familiar tune. For instance if children made peanut butter and cracker sandwiches, encourage them to recall the steps in the process, and turn their words into a song. For example, chant, or sing to the tune of the common preschool song "Peanut Butter and Jelly,"

> First, we took the knife and
> We scooped it, we scooped it.
> Next we took the cracker and
> We spread it, we spread it.

2 Ask children to pretend they are certain foods that are going through the process of being prepared or cooked. Begin by using foods that were part of children's real or pretend cooking experiences. For example, on the day Elyse pretended to cook scrambled eggs, her teacher asked the children to pretend they were scrambled eggs cooking in a pan. Then the teacher encouraged the children to suggest other food experiences for the group to act out.

Eating

3 Fill a basket with crackers and make a game of passing it. Play a musical selection (for example, "Hot Pretzels" from Volume 8 of High/Scope's *Rhythmically Moving* recording series) and have the children sit in a large circle and pass the basket around the circle. When the music stops the person left holding the basket eats a cracker. Make sure to end the game with a cracker break for everyone.

4 Sing familiar songs, asking children to sing as if they have various foods in their mouths. For example, as children sing "Twinkle, Twinkle, Little Star," you might

ask them

- "Pretend your mouth is full of peanut butter."
- "Pretend you have grapes stuffed inside one of your cheeks."
- "Pretend you are chewing on a piece of bubblegum."

Ask children to suggest their own ideas for the group to try.

What We Learned From Our Observations of Children

After implementing the above teaching strategies, adults recorded anecdotal notes describing their observations. A sample of these anecdotes is presented in "Child Observations" on pages 141–143. The teachers used the High/Scope Child Observation Record (COR) to help them interpret the children's behaviors according to a developmental framework. Each anecdote is presented here with the COR item and level the teachers matched it with.

Adult Training Activities

This training activity is designed to encourage teaching teams to examine their own beliefs about food and how these affect the ways they interact with children during food-related experiences.

1. With participants grouped by teaching team, distribute the following discussion sheet to each team and ask team members to discuss their personal reactions to the situations described. Each teaching team should note their answers to the questions given in the space provided.

Scenario One:

> *Mashed potatoes are served with the school lunch. While sitting at the table, you notice that Mary is not eating the potatoes. Instead, she is absorbed in making gullies in the potatoes with the bottom of her spoon and watching the way the gravy moves back and forth between the gullies. Lunch is almost over and she is still playing with her food rather than eating it.*

> What would you do?

Scenario Two:

The day after Halloween, Madison brings a bag of her Halloween candy to school. You tell her to put it inside her cubbie and keep it there until it is time to go home. She does, but then at work time you notice Madison and three other children huddled in a corner of the room eating chocolate bars and lollipops.

What would you do?

Scenario Three:

Lunch time seems to have gotten chaotic at your preschool. Children sit wherever they want, exchange food with one another, and never say please or thank you.

What would you do?

Scenario Four:

While pretending to have a dinner party, two of the girls talk about inviting their "boyfriends." They set the table with a tablecloth and candlesticks and then tell you they are drinking margaritas and wine.

What would you do?

2. After team members have recorded their reactions and answers, ask them to examine and discuss their suggested actions in terms of who (child or adult) is in control of the situation and what kinds of learning will take place.

Child Observations

INITIATIVE

TEACHER'S ANECDOTAL NOTES	HIGH/SCOPE COR ITEM AND LEVEL
At planning time Taryn took the spatula and pointed it toward the art area. She then left the table and began painting at the easel.	A. Expressing choices: (2) Child indicates a desired activity or place of activity by saying a word, pointing, or some other action.
At work time Jordan picked up the cheese grater, rubbed the cheese across it one time, and looked underneath. "No cheese," he said, then left the cooking table.	B. Solving problems: (2) Child identifies problems, but does not try to solve them, turning instead to another activity.
At work time Leah took the magazine pictures of food and used the scissors to cut fringes around the edges of the paper.	C. Engaging in complex play: (2) Child shows interest in simple use of materials or simple participation in activities.
At work time Emma paged through the food magazines. She cut out pictures of food and placed them in two piles. Then she got glue and construction paper and drew a line down the middle of a piece of construction paper. She pasted pictures from one pile on one side of the paper, those from the other pile, on the other side. Then she told her teacher, "These are foods I like and these I don't like."	C. Engaging in complex play: (4) Child, acting alone, carries out complex and varied sequences of activities.
After lunch, Sue told Malinda [a teacher] that she was not going to brush her teeth today because her Daddy said she didn't have to and she didn't like the toothpaste taste.	D. Cooperating in program routines: (2) Child sometimes follows program routines.

SOCIAL RELATIONS

TEACHER'S ANECDOTAL NOTES	HIGH/SCOPE COR ITEM AND LEVEL
At work time when Ann [a teacher] asked Howard to pass her the ladle he said, "Oh, I'm not supposed to because it might be hot.	E. Relating to adults: (2) Child responds when familiar adults initiate interactions.
At work time Min spent 45 minutes planning a "dinner party" with Andrea. First, they visited the grocery store to "buy the food," then they "cooked" it, then they set the table with a tablecloth and candles in the candlestick holders.	F. Relating to other children: (5) Child works on complex projects with other children.
At lunch, when Jeremy called Taryn a baby because she spilled her milk, Tanuka said, "She's not a baby. It was just a spill and everybody spills."	G. Making friends with other children: (5) Child appears to receive social support from a friend and shows loyalty to the friend.

Continued on the next page.

Continued from the previous page.

TEACHER'S ANECDOTAL NOTES	HIGH/SCOPE COR ITEM AND LEVEL
Frederick said to Malinda [a teacher] at small-group time, "Help me get some of the sesame seeds before Min uses them up."	H. Engaging in social problem solving: (3) Child requests adult help in solving problems with other children.
At small-group time Jamie watched Min pick up a teddy bear counter with chopsticks. Then he tried it. When he couldn't get the chopsticks to work, he pushed all the toys off the table and screamed, "I can't."	I. Understanding and expressing feelings: (2) Child expresses or verbalizes feelings, but sometimes in unacceptable ways.

CREATIVE REPRESENTATION

TEACHER'S ANECDOTAL NOTES	HIGH/SCOPE COR ITEM AND LEVEL
At work time Diana took two octagon blocks from the block puzzle, stacked them sandwich-style, then sat at the house area table pretending to takes bites from them.	J. Making and building: (4) Child uses materials to make a simple representation and says or demonstrates what it is.
At planning time, Jamie drew a picture of a yellow wedge of cheese and a cheese grater. The drawing of the cheese grater showed a handle on top of an oblong rectangle. Inside the rectangle were rows of circles. Jamie said his plan was to "grate cheese."	K. Drawing or painting: (5) Child draws or paints representations with many details.
At large-group time, Jeremy muffled his voice while singing, pretending there was peanut butter stuck in his mouth.	L. Pretending: (2) Child uses one object to stand for another or uses actions or sounds to pretend.
At planning time, Kayla walked around the table with a note pad, saying, "May I please take your planning order." As each child told her where he was going to play, she made marks on the pad before going on to another person.	L. Pretending: (3) Child assumes the role of someone or something else, or talks in language appropriate to the assumed role.

MUSIC AND MOVEMENT

TEACHER'S ANECDOTAL NOTES	HIGH/SCOPE COR ITEM AND LEVEL
At work time Madison filled a wok with "food" and carried it in one hand from the house area to the block area without spilling the contents.	M. Exhibiting body coordination: (4) Child moves around while manipulating an object.
At small-group time David strung Cheerios on pipe cleaners, filling three pipe cleaners.	N. Exhibiting manual coordination: (4) Child manipulates small objects with precision.
At work time, while listening to a tape and cooking dinner for a "dinner party," Andrea tapped the wooden spoon against the pot to the beat of the music.	O. Imitating movements to a steady beat: (3) Child responds to the beat of songs or instrumental music with simple movements.

LANGUAGE AND LITERACY

Teacher's Anecdotal Notes	*High/Scope COR Item and Level*
At planning time when Kayla said, "May I please take your planning order?" Alex said, "to the block area."	Q. Understanding speech: (3) Child responds to simple, direct, conversational sentences.
At work time, when she had finished eating crackers, Tanuka prepared the eating space for the next child by covering the crackers, throwing away her napkin, and washing and drying the table, as Malinda [a teacher] had suggested.	Q. Understanding speech: (5) Child follows multistep or complex directions.
At recall, when pretending to be in line at the "drive-through," Andrea told the person pretending to be the restaurant employee, "At work time I had a dinner party and made delicious food to eat by candlelight with my new boyfriend."	R. Speaking: (4) Child uses sentences that include two or more ideas with descriptive details.
When pretending to look at the menu to order food at work time Michael pointed to the **H** and said, "That says **H.** I'll have a hamburger."	U. Beginning reading: (2) Child identifies some letters and numbers.
As she takes children's planning orders Kayla writes "BLK," "ART," and "TOY" on her pad.	V. Beginning writing: (4) Child writes some words or short phrases besides own name.

LOGIC AND MATHEMATICS

Teacher's Anecdotal Notes	*High/Scope COR Item and Level*
Madison pours an assortment of small items into a large saucepan and calls them "lunch." Then she puts the straws on one plate and calls them "macaroni" and the buttons on another and calls them "Cheerios."	W. Sorting: (2) Child groups identical objects together.
At work time, as Andrea and Min were discussing the preparations for their pretend dinner party, Andrea said, "Look at all the food I got from the store—some fruits, some vegetables, and some eggs."	X. Using the words *not, some,* and *all:* (5) Child distinguishes between *some,* and *all* and uses these terms in categorizing.
At small-group time, while scooping out the insides of a cooked squash, Madison said, "The hot oven is what made this skin softer than before."	Z. Using comparison words: (4) Child uses comparison words correctly.
At work time Min set the table for four people: herself, Andrea, and their two boyfriends. She provided a cup, plate, and spoon for each person. "Everyone has three," she says.	AA. Comparing numbers of objects: (3) Child correctly judges whether two groups of up to five objects each contain the same number of objects.
At small-group time Jeremy told Michael, "If you want to get the cheese out of the box, you have to turn it upside down and shake it."	CC. Describing spatial relations: Child uses words that describe the direction of movement of things.

Character Play 9

Pooh,

Piglet, and

Power Rangers

Trey and Glen, who ride to school together every day and occasionally visit each other on the weekends, arrive at school Monday morning after a particularly snowy weekend. Glen is holding the storybook **The Snowman** by Raymond Briggs. He explains to his teacher, Malinda, that he and Trey watched the videotaped version of **The Snowman** over the weekend. "It's like this book, but it has music and the pictures move around." Malinda sits next to Trey and Glen at greeting time and watches as they go through **The Snowman** page by page, comparing what happens in the book to what happens in the videotape. Some of their comments include "This is where he shushes the snowman because Mommy and Daddy are sleeping." "Children should never get into freezers because they could suffocate." "Look out, rabbit, the motorcycle is coming through really fast. Now it's going faster." "The boy feels sad because the snowman is gone."

That morning during outside time, Glen and Trey ask Malinda if she will help them make "a really tall snowman like in the story." The two boys work together with Malinda until they have a tall snowman; then the boys go inside to search for things that can be used for the snowman's features. They come out with two Bristle Blocks to serve as the eyes, a magic marker for the nose, yarn for hair, and a strip of paper for the mouth. When the snowman is completed, Glen steps back from it, looks up at Malinda and says, "I wish this snowman could fly me in the air like in the videotape."

"Hi, I'm Rabbit," says Tanuka to Michael as she sits down at the lunch table across from him. "You be Piglet, Sue is Pooh and Stephanie is Tigger." Tanuka continues, "We have to teach Christopher Robin about good manners and how to dance so he can go to the party." Sue, who has been listening to Tanuka, responds, "Party, party, Rabbit. Did I hear someone say party?"

Throughout lunch, Tanuka continues to call children by the names of **Winnie-the-Pooh** *characters. After rest time, Tanuka makes a plan to have a party with her Pooh friends at afternoon work time. After setting the table in the house area, she calls to Michael, Sue, and Stephanie (using their* **Pooh***-character names) and invites them over to the table. When they children arrive, Tanuka begins instructing them in how to eat, reminding them that they must take only small portions and say please and thank you. When the meal is over she tells them, "It's time to learn how to dance." She gets a doll from the baby bed for them to hold as they practice their steps. While she is singing "One and, two and, three," Michael runs and gets a drum and beats in time to her voice.*

Later, at outside time, Tanuka rolls two tires into a corner of the playground. She places a large round Tinkertoy piece in the middle of each tire, plants a Tinkertoy stick in it, and drapes a blanket over the stick. When the blanket falls off, she heads into the classroom to get masking tape. When she returns, she asks her friends to help her secure the blanket to the Tinkertoy stick "so Christopher Robin's new, bigger house will have a roof." As they work, she assures her friends, "Don't worry, at the end he still plays with us even though he's growing up." When her father comes to pick Tanuka up, the teacher tells him about his daughter's character play. Tanuka's father explains that she received a videotape about Winnie-the-Pooh two weeks ago as a birthday gift and has been watching it several times a day ever since. He says that Tanuka's play at home is much the same as at school, and he describes how she assigns family members different roles and gets quite upset if they call her Tanuka instead of Rabbit.

☙

It is work time in the block area, and Daniel and Victor make a long line of card-board-brick blocks across the floor. Daniel then gets out two wooden unit blocks while Victor goes to the art area and brings back construction paper, tape, scissors, and markers. They meet back at their original structure and begin cutting pieces of the construction paper into small irregular shapes. Using the tape, they fasten the paper pieces to the tops of the long wooden unit blocks. After all this preparation, they call Barbara, their teacher, over to the block area "to help make the arrows and the numbers." "You want help with arrows and numbers?" she says. "Yes," says Victor, "so we can change the channels." Barbara questions them about what numbers they want and which direction the arrows should point. "We need a three," says Daniel, "because that's the VCR number." "You have to make one this way and the other that way," says Victor, pointing his fingers in opposite directions. "Also, don't forget to make the one for fast-forward. That's a double," he adds.

When the arrows and numbers are completed, Daniel and Victor sit down on the cardboard blocks, facing the block storage shelf, and point to and press the num-

bers on their "remote controls." They invite Barbara to come and watch television with them, telling her "It's Saturday, you know, and we're watching cartoons." They sit side by side clicking their switches and giggling at the pretend television screen. Between channel switches, they jump up and do a "fancy footwork" routine, swinging their arms and legs in pretend kicks and punches and rolling on the ground. They never actually touch each other in this make-believe fight. They explain that they are "the Power Rangers" and they are "fighting the bad guys." They then sit back down and pretend to insert a videotape in their "VCR." Victor tells Daniel, who is now holding one of the remote controls, "Press fast-forward so we can skip the previews."

Who's Coming to School This Morning? What Children Learn From Character Play

Whether we approve or not, most children spend many hours each week watching television programs and movies. They often become absorbed in a make-believe world peopled by a range of television and movie characters, and they are fond of re-enacting the language and behaviors of these characters in their play. Many children are equally attached to particular characters they've encountered in storybooks, and such favorite characters also appear quite often in their play. The frequent availability of both book and video versions of the same story often heightens children's interest in particular characters.

Listening carefully to children as they describe their favorite characters from television, stories, or movies will give you valuable information about their ideas and interests.

Many adults feel young children spend too much time viewing television programs, videotapes, and movies; they also question whether the content of these programs is appropriate for children. Thus they may be reluctant to encourage or build on children's interest in television and movie characters when it arises in the classroom. When a child is interested in fantasy characters from children's literature, however, most adults are comfortable in supporting this interest. Whatever your personal reactions may be to television or movies, it's important to recognize that fantasy characters, whatever their source, are an important interest of children. As with any strong interest, children's fascination with these characters can be a vehicle for learning.

Supporting Children's Interest in Fantasy Characters

When adults suspend judgment about the content of children's spontaneous character play, they often are surprised at how many learning experiences they observe during such play. On pages 150–151 are some of the observations adults recorded about individual children while observing the play experiences that open this chapter. To highlight the learning experiences that were occurring, adults classified these anecdotes according to the High/Scope key experience categories. The strategies teachers developed for supporting further learning for these children and their classmates are presented next.

General Teaching and Interaction Strategies

✔ **Ask parents for information about the videotapes or movies their children are watching outside of school hours so you are familiar with the interests children are enacting in their play.** One teaching team asked parents to fill out a simple

Children use a wide range of abilities in character play. Here Audie and James have devised a turn-taking game involving favorite characters.

Steps in Conflict Resolution

1   **Approach calmly.** Your body language says a lot about your intentions and feelings. Stay neutral in order to respect all the points of view.

2   **Acknowledge feelings.** Make simple statements, such as "I can see you're feeling sad/angry/upset." This helps the child let go of feelings and prepares him/her to think clearly about solutions.

3   **Gather information.** Listen to all points of view, both for your own information and so children can learn what others believe they need. The details revealed about the conflict are very important in finding a solution. Listen carefully.

4   **Restate the problem.** Use as much of the children's language as possible and rephrase child language that may be hurtful.

5   **Ask for ideas for solutions and choose one together.** Respect all of the children's ideas, even if some are unrealistic. Explore how each idea might work, considering the consequences. Help children think through the specifics of very general solutions such as "They can share."

6   **Be prepared to give follow-up support.** Sometimes children need further help in clarifying the details of a solution.

questionnaire about their children's favorite entertainment. The questionnaire asked for plot summaries, a list of the main characters' names, and descriptions of the parts of these programs and movies that their children particularly enjoyed.

✔ **Borrow or rent videos of interest to your children for your own viewing;** this will enable you to participate more fully when video-related play surfaces in the classroom.

✔ **Support children's interest in fantasy characters by talking to them in the pretend role they have assumed.** When Tanuka took on the part of Rabbit from *Winnie-the-Pooh,* her teachers addressed her as Rabbit at her request, for example, (at lunch time) "Rabbit, please pass me a napkin," and (at recall time) "Rabbit, what did you do during work time today?" When teachers or other children slipped and called her by her real name, Tanuka was quick to point out that she was "Rabbit today, not Tanuka."

✔ **Examine your own views about video and television watching; avoid letting your opinions interfere with your ability to support children** when they express their interests in video and television themes. Although Victor and Daniel's teacher Barbara was not a supporter of the Power Ranger program and the message it sends, she did not squelch the play behaviors she observed in Daniel and Victor simply because they were connected to this program.

✔ **If you feel that children's imitation of television and video violence is leading to conflict and disruption in your classroom, use a problem-solving process to**

When conflicts arise because character play gets too loud or rough, help children think through the problem before resuming play.

Child Observations

CREATIVE REPRESENTATION

At work time Tanuka set the table and called three of her friends over "to share some food." As they "ate," she made comments about their table manners: "No, no, only take small bites." "Remember to say please and thank you." When they finished eating, she gave each child a turn dancing with a baby doll, so they could "learn how to dance."

In the block area at work time, Daniel and Victor imitated the actions of Power Ranger characters, making punching and kicking motions with their hands and feet, then rolling on the ground.

At outside time Trey and Glen went inside the classroom to collect materials for decorating their snowman. They returned with Bristle Blocks for the eyes, a marker for the nose, yarn for the hair, and a paper strip for the mouth.

LANGUAGE AND LITERACY

At greeting circle Trey and Glen sat next to Malinda [a teacher] and took turns "picture-reading" **The Snowman.**

When explaining to Barbara [a teacher] how to make a fast-forward button for a remote control, Victor said "That's a double."

INITIATIVE AND SOCIAL RELATIONS

At lunch, Sue heard Tanuka calling herself Rabbit and talking about teaching Christopher Robin table manners so he could go to a party. Sue responded, "Party, party, Rabbit. Did I hear someone say **party**?"

At outside time, after building and decorating a snowman, Glen said, "I wish this snowman could fly me in the air like in the videotape."

Daniel and Victor spent all of work time in the block area making a pretend television with remote-control channel-switchers. After they completed it, they sat side by side clicking their controls and giggling at the make-believe screen.

At greeting circle, while narrating the book **The Snowman** for Malinda, Glen said, "The boy feels sad because the snowman is gone."

MOVEMENT

When Barbara [a teacher] asked Victor how he could make an arrow for his remote control, he pointed his fingers in opposite directions and said, "You have to make one this way and the other that way."

At outside time Tanuka rolled two tires to a corner of the playground so she could build a "new, bigger house for Christopher Robin."

MUSIC

As she gave dance lessons to her friends, Tanuka chanted, "One and, two and, three."

As Michael and Tanuka taught their friends to dance, Michael beat a drum in time with Tanuka as she chanted "One and, two and, three."

CLASSIFICATION

At work time, when Daniel asked Barbara [a teacher] for help in making a remote-control, he said, "We need a three because that's the VCR number."

*Describing the difference between the book and videotape versions of **The Snowman,** Glen said, "It's like this book, but it has music and the pictures move around."*

SERIATION

*While "picture-reading" **The Snowman** to Malinda [a teacher] at greeting circle, Trey said, "Look out, rabbit, the motorcycle is coming through really fast. Now it's going faster."*

NUMBER

At work time Tanuka set the table with four place settings, then called three of her friends over to join her in sharing food for the party.

At outside time Trey and Glen got two blocks for their snowman's eyes, one strip of paper for the mouth, and one magic marker for the nose.

SPACE

At work time, as they punched, kicked, and rolled on the ground pretending to be Power Rangers, Daniel and Victor danced around each other without making physical contact.

At outside time Tanuka used tires, large Tinkertoy blocks, a blanket, and masking tape to make an enclosed space with a "roof" on the top.

TIME

*Several times during the day Tanuka acted out a sequence from a **Winnie-the-Pooh** videotape in which a meal is served, dancing is taught, and a new, bigger house is built for Christopher Robin.*

While pretending to watch television in the block area during work time, Victor said to Barbara [a teacher], "It's Saturday, you know, and we're watching cartoons."

resolve conflicts that arise. In addition, make efforts to educate parents about the negative impact of exposure to this kind of entertainment. To support children's conflict resolution, use the six-step process described in the box on page 149. (This process and other ideas for dealing with superhero play are presented in High/Scope *Extensions*, March/April 1995.)

✔ **Let children's play unfold even when you are not sure of the direction it is taking.** While it was impossible for Barbara to know what Victor and Daniel were doing when they gathered all their materials for their VCR-building activity and subsequent Power Ranger play, she did not get involved until they called her over and requested help with the arrows and numbers. Then she simply reflected back their requests until they clearly spelled out their ideas for making a remote control for their VCR. In the same situation, another teacher might have stepped in when she saw the boys using tape with the blocks ("Blocks are for building and tape might ruin them") or when the boys started their pretend fight. However, in both these instances, Barbara resisted the temptation to get involved. In the first instance she realized that, although it was unusual to use tape with blocks, this really wouldn't harm the blocks. Similarly, when she observed the boys' pretend punching and kicking, she saw that they were quite skilled in avoiding actions that might be hurtful; she also observed that the pretend fighting was not interfering with other children's play.

Indoor and Outdoor Materials to Add

Snow and snowmen

1 When children bring in or otherwise express interest in particular stories, provide related books to build on this interest. To support Trey and Glen's interest in comparing and narrating different versions of *The Snowman,* the teachers added storybooks about snow and snowmen to the book area and observed whether Trey and Glen continued to retell, make up, and compare related stories. One book they added, *Sadie and the Snowman* by Allan Morgan, gave Trey and Glen additional ideas about things they could use to add features to their snowmen; it also gave them another way to experience the feelings associated with snowmen melting. In addition, to help the other children understand Trey and Glen's discussions and related role play about *The Snowman,* the teachers introduced the original story to other children in the class whenever the opportunity arose.

2 If children have been building real snowmen outdoors, add materials to the art area so they can create "snowmen" inside the classroom. Possible materials include Styrofoam balls and white paper circles in various sizes, cotton balls, and white chalk. Encourage children to compare their outdoor creations to the snowmen they make with these materials and the snowmen in books and videotapes.

3 Fill the sand and water table with snow, and encourage children to compare their indoor and outdoor snow experiences.

4 To build on children's interest in comparing different versions of the same story, stock your book area with the same stories in different formats. For example *The Very Hungry Caterpillar* comes in small- and large-sized versions, as does *Who's in the Shed?* by Brenda Parkes. Some books, especially children's classics such as *Winnie-the-Pooh,* are available both in "chapter-book" and shortened versions. If you know that children have been watching particular videotapes at home (such as the video series corresponding to chapters in the original *Winnie-the-Pooh*), add the corresponding book version of the story to the book area.

5 If children have been enjoying "picture-reading" familiar books (narrating the story in their own words while looking at the pictures) or if you have observed them comparing different versions of favorite stories, provide additional narration and comparison experiences by taking photos of individual children at work time and mounting them together in a book (see strategy 2, "Planning and Recall Experiences," page 155). Ask children to dictate captions about what is happening in the pictures and write down their words in the book. Add this book to the book area. Later when children "read" it, encourage them to make "then and now" comparisons: Is the clothing they are wearing now different from the clothing shown in the pictures? Have they grown since the photos were taken? Are they now playing in new ways with the materials shown in the pictures?

Pooh *characters*

6 To encourage children to recall details about favorite storybook characters, add audiovisual materials related to the story to the classroom. For example, to build on Tanuka's interest in *Winnie-the-Pooh* characters, the teachers made tape recordings of some of her favorite *Pooh* stories and added them to the book area with the books themselves. When you make story tapes like these, vary the format. Include some tapes that are simply straight narrations of the stories and others in which you occasionally depart from the story to ask a question or make a comment about something shown on a page from the book. This gives children opportunities to talk about the story in their own words.

7 When you observe children role-playing various storybook characters, add related props to encourage them to extend their role play. These may include actual replicas of the desired characters or similar, less expensive, toys that children can use to represent the characters. Tanuka's teachers added stuffed animals similar to the Pooh characters—a bear, a donkey, a pig, a rabbit, and a kangaroo—to the book area. They also added a pot labeled with the word "HUNNY" (as spelled in the book) to the house area and a cardboard owl (covered with Con-Tact paper to withstand various weather conditions) to a favorite tree in the outdoor play area.

VCRs *and superheroes*

8 To build on children's interest in televisions and VCRs, add old remote control units, empty plastic videotape boxes, and old videotapes to the block area.

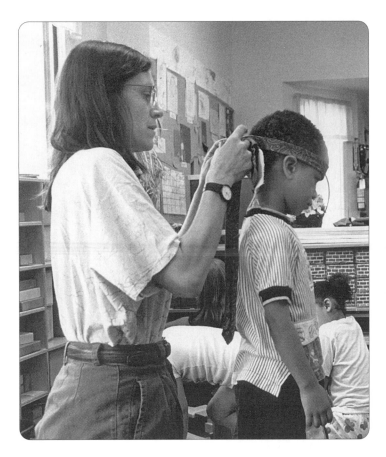

The availability of character-related materials encourages children to expand and add detail to their character play.

9   Sometimes children, like Victor and Daniel, engage in video- and television-related role play that involves the use of remote control units, fast-forward buttons, and so forth. Children's fascination with such devices often seems to stem from their interest in manipulating and controlling their entertainment selections; children are aware that these gadgets enable viewers to choose what they will watch and when (for example, press this button and a certain television show comes on, press the fast-forward button and you can skip the commercials). If you observe this interest in your group of children, you can provide opportunities for similar kinds of experiences by adding a real tape recorder to your classroom. Also, provide old tapes so children can experiment with all the buttons and controls without fear of erasing the tapes.

10   Add materials and props children can use to dress up as their favorite television and video characters. For example, to enable Daniel and Victor to expand on their Power Ranger play, the teachers added to the house area all-one-color sweatsuits in several colors, scarves, boots, headbands, gloves, and karate belts, as well as tin foil for making head gear, scrap fabric for making capes, and materials such as paper-towel tubes and PVC piping for making other superhero accessories.

11   If children, like Victor and Daniel, have been enjoying pretend kicking and punching, add materials that will provide opportunities for other kinds of large-motor movement. Tumbling mats, large ribbon rings, punching bags, and parachutes are some examples of materials that inspire a range of movement experiences.

Planning and Recall Experiences

Snow and snowmen

1   When you hear children talking about, retelling, and comparing stories from videotapes or storybooks, use their ideas and language in your planning and recall strategies. To highlight Trey and Glen's interpretations of and reflections on *The Snowman* book, their teacher brought a snowman prop to the planning/recall table and asked the children to let the snowman fly them to their work time destinations. For recall time that day, she made a similar reference to Trey and Glen's interest in the motorcycle in *The Snowman,* suggesting to the children, "Pretend you are on the fast motorcycle in *The Snowman,* race to the area you worked in, then race back to the table to describe your work to the others."

2   Capitalize on the children's interest in "picture-reading" by taking instant photographs of children during work time. Bring the pictures to the recall table and ask children to describe to the others what they were doing in the pictures. As children get older and their descriptions become more detailed, you can turn this into a guessing game—ask one child at a time to describe the actions of others in the group, and ask the rest of the children to guess, by looking at the pictures, who the child is talking about.

Pooh *characters*

3   Integrate into your planning and recall strategies props that are similar to objects in children's favorite stories. For example, for a Pooh-related planning or recall session, set a pot in the middle of the table labeled with the word "HUNNY" as in the book. Lay out interest area symbol cards or objects from the areas, and provide a stuffed bear for the child who is planning or recalling. (If possible, use an actual replica of Pooh Bear.) The child with the bear picks the symbol or object for the area he or she plans to work in (or has worked in) and tosses it into the honey pot. The child then describes his or her ideas to the others, pretending that it is the bear who is doing the talking.

4   Take the children outside for recall time and have them gather around the tree where the cardboard owl is hanging (see strategy 7, "Indoor and Outdoor Materials to Add," page 153). Ask children to tell Owl a story about what happened inside during work time. Bring materials that you saw children using (for example, a paintbrush) so they can act out some of the motions of the activities they are describing. Or bring *Pooh*-character stuffed animals outside "to talk to Owl."

5   Ask children to pretend to be a favorite character that you have observed children imitating in the classroom, and to move to their chosen work areas as that character. In Tanuka's classroom, the teachers asked children to hop to the area they planned to work in while pretending to be Rabbit from *Winnie-the-Pooh*. At recall time the whole group used a similar strategy. The first child to recall hopped like

Rabbit to the area she worked in, with the rest of the group hopping after her. The group sat there and listened as the children who worked in that area recalled their experiences. Then the group hopped to the area of the next child's experiences and repeated the process.

VCRs and superheroes

6   Make a pretend remote control by taping pieces of paper to a piece of wood, using small area symbols as the control buttons. Ask the children one by one to point the remote control at their chosen work area, to click the button representing the area, and then to describe the actions they are planning or recalling.

7   Cut out a cardboard box so that it looks like a television screen, making the hole large enough for a child's face to be seen through the opening. Make a pretend remote control marked with numbers to represent channels on the television. Give a number to each child at the beginning of planning or recall. Ask the child with the remote control to pick a number that someone is holding, and to "tune in" to that station. The child selected is the next to plan or recall. As children describe plans or experiences, they put the box over their heads so they are "on television."

A simple prop turns this planning time into an extension of children's earlier work time activities revolving around television and VCRs.

8 Give the child who is planning or recalling a superhero prop (a karate belt, headband, wristband, or cape) to wear while describing his or her plans or experiences.

Active superhero play is one way children express their need for large-motor movement. To provide another outlet for children's physical energy, plan a physically active recall time.

Small-Group Experiences

Snow and snowmen

1 To build on children's interest in narrating stories as they page through a favorite book ("picture-reading"), bring a storybook featuring a similar topic to the small group. (In Glen and Trey's class, teachers used a book about snow.) Together with the children, read the book, encouraging the children to act out parts and add their own narration. When you finish reading the book have materials available that children may use to create their own story illustrations (for example, snow-related materials might be added, such as those listed in strategy 2, "Indoor and Outdoor Materials to Add," page 152). Then suggest that children tell the story that goes with the picture or pictures they have made. Take dictation at children's request (some children may prefer to "write" and "read" their own stories or may consider the pictures themselves a type of writing). Encourage children to compare their own stories with the one just read.

2 Visit the local library and arrange for the librarian to read or tell a different version of a familiar book you have in your book area at school. For example, there are many versions of *The Three Little Pigs*. After the trip tell or read both versions again with the children. Listen for children's comments to see if children compare the two versions of the story, as Trey and Glen compared the print and video versions of *The Snowman*.

3 For each child, provide a set of stickers and ink stamps representing similar items (animals, foods, vehicles); an ink pad; and paper cut and folded to make a small, blank book. As children create their own pictures and stories, listen as they comment on the differences between the stickers and the stamps.

Pooh *characters*

4 If you have observed children acting out stories from books or videotapes, as Tanuka and her friends did, give children an opportunity to re-enact familiar stories using small toys. For each child, prepare a basket containing small building blocks and tiny animal figures similar to the Winnie-the-Pooh characters (or other toy figures similar to characters from another book your children are interested in). Before distributing the materials tell a *short* story based on the story-inspired play

you have observed, using the materials in one of the baskets to demonstrate the actions and language of the characters. Then pass out a set of materials to each child and watch and listen as they create their own stories.

5 Purchase or make ink stamps (see strategy 5, "Small-Group Experiences," Chapter 4, page 61) to represent the characters in one of children's favorite stories (for example, *Winnie-the-Pooh*). Give each child paper, stamps, and ink pads to create a personal story. Include markers and crayons so children can add additional details to the stamp-made pictures. Take dictation from children at their request, and support any other ways they choose to "write" in their books. (Some children may consider their pictures as writing.)

VCRs and superheroes

6 If children, like Victor and Daniel, have been engaging in pretend fighting, take the small group outside to a space where they can safely roll on the ground and pretend to kick and punch (this activity is enhanced if a hill is available for children to roll down). You can also make available as props a variety of balls for kicking and padded gloves for children to wear while punching in the air. To introduce this activity say something like this: "Yesterday at work time I saw Victor and Daniel pretending to be Power Rangers. They were moving their arms and legs without touching each other. Here are some things you can use as you move your arms and legs." Some children may enjoy play fighting while others may prefer rolling down the hill and playing with balls.

As they collect trash on a walk around the neighborhood, these children are imitating the environmental cleanup activities of favorite television characters.

7 Read stories to the children that involve themes of power, control, and mastering fear. Two examples are *There's a Nightmare in My Closet* by Mercer Mayer and *The Monster Bed* by Jeanne Willis. As you read the story, be alert to children's concerns and comments about the feelings depicted and the ways the fears described were resolved by the characters in the book. After reading the book, give children open-ended building or art materials and encourage them to create something that will protect them from monsters or anything else inspired by the story.

8 Provide a paper or plastic trash bag for each child in the small group. Engage children in a discussion of the environmental cleanup aspects of the *Power Ranger* program. After the discussion, take them outside for a trash-collecting walk. When you get back, encourage children to compare what they collected on their walk.

9 To build on children's interest in pretend martial arts, take a field trip to a local karate studio or an indoor gym play structure.

Large-Group Experiences

Snow and snowmen

1 Ask children to share their ideas about the ways the pictures in a favorite story-book could be acted out, then imitate those actions. In Trey and Glen's classroom, the children suggested the following ideas from *The Snowman:* "Pretend you are riding on the back of a fast motorcycle as you run around the circle," "Put on capes and pretend you are flying in the air," "Put on music and dance the way the snowmen do in a large circle," "Pretend you are a snowman melting," "Pretend you feel sad because the snowman is gone." If your children are old enough to understand this, you can ask them first to imitate the actions as they would appear in the video version (with movement and sound) and then to freeze like statues of the characters.

Pooh *characters*

2 Record the soundtrack from video versions of familiar books you see children retelling in the classroom. Have children move to that music at large-group time. Ask children for their ideas about ways to move (for example, bouncing, with scarves, tapping chopsticks in different places).

Children use stuffed bears to tap the steady beat to their favorite Winnie-the-Pooh music.

3 Pick songs that are sung on the video-tape versions of familiar books and sing them with the children. Change the lyrics to include the children's own names or ideas. For example, Tanuka's teachers learned the song "The Wonderful Thing About Tigger" from one of the *Pooh* videos (available on the audio cassette, *Winnie-the-Pooh Music Sampler,* Walt Disney Co. Records). After singing it with the whole group as it is performed in the video version, they changed the words to "The Wonderful Thing About . . ." then inserted the children's names. As their names came up, individual children, or their friends, would describe a wonderful thing about that person that would become the next verse of the song.

VCRs and superheroes

4 If children have been imitating superheroes in the classroom and, like Audie and James in Chapter 5, are ready to explore games with rules, play games that provide

another kind of opportunity for experiencing power and control. One example is a variation of the common game Duck, Duck, Goose. Divide the group into two small circles, so children have a shorter waiting time than is usual with this game. One child walks around the circle tapping others on the head while repeating a phrase that she has chosen; the child who is last to be tapped jumps up and chases after the first child until they come around to the empty spot. Then the first person to chant sits down, the new person repeats the process of chanting and tapping, and so on. Some of the chants used might include "Duck, duck, duck, goose"; "Hot dog, hot dog, hot dog, French Fries"; Power Ranger, Power Ranger, Power Ranger, bad guy."

5 If children have been making and using make-believe television remote controls, use one of these as a prop during transitions to or from the large-group activity. Give one child the remote control, and have that child click it while pointing to the next person to leave the activity. The chosen person clicks at one child at a time until all children are gone.

6 If children have been swinging their arms and legs in pretend fighting, play games that enable them to exercise the same muscles. For example, provide a large parachute or bed sheet. Have children run in a circle while hanging on to the parachute or sheet with one hand. Or, have them stand still while holding the cloth in both hands. Then ask them to raise and lower the cloth, using large, sweeping arm movements.

What We Learned From Our Observations of Children

After the teaching strategies described in this chapter were tried, teachers observed a wide range of learning experiences in their classrooms and centers. To interpret these experiences, the teachers used the High/Scope Child Observation Record (COR) as a developmental framework. A sampling of the anecdotal notes and the corresponding High/Scope COR items the teachers matched them with is presented in "Child Observations," on the next three pages.

For the first time, Mark ties his superhero scarf without an adult's help.

Child Observations

INITIATIVE

TEACHER'S ANECDOTAL NOTES	*HIGH/SCOPE COR ITEM AND LEVEL*
I'm going to stick the tape in there," said Adam as he pointed to the tape recorder, "so I can hear Julie sing."	A. Expressing choices: (4) Child indicates with a short sentence how plans will be carried out.
"Let's play catch," Kacey said to Julia at small-group time. You roll the ball down the hill to me, and I'll get it and roll it up to you."	A. Expressing choices: (5) Child gives detailed description of intended actions.
At work time Micah tried to fit the videotape into its paper jacket. She inserted it lengthwise, instead of by the short end. When this didn't work, she dropped it on the floor.	B. Solving problems: (3) Child uses one method to try to solve a problem, but if unsuccessful, gives up after one or two tries.
At work time Kacey sorted through the white circles. She picked three different-sized circles, glued them to a piece of construction paper, then covered them with cotton balls. Finally she used a piece of white chalk to make dots all around the snowman and explained, "It's snowing so he won't melt."	C. Engaging in complex play: (3) Child, acting alone, uses materials or organizes active play involving two or more steps.

SOCIAL RELATIONS

TEACHER'S ANECDOTAL NOTES	*HIGH/SCOPE COR ITEM AND LEVEL*
At naptime, while other children were resting, Ruthi helped Stephanie [an adult] cover the paper owl with Con-Tact paper and punch a hole in it for hanging in the tree. She went outside with Stephanie and passed the owl up to her for tying to the tree branch.	E. Relating to adults: (5) Child works on complex projects with familiar adults.
At large-group time Sue pointed the pretend remote control at Tanuka and said, "I'm picking Tanuka because she is my best friend."	G. Making friends with other children: (3) Child identifies a classmate as a friend.
When Tanuka yelled, "You have to be Piglet, because that's what I want," Michael went up to Stephanie [a teacher] and said, "You tell her I don't want to play."	H. Engaging in social problem solving: (3) Child requests adult help in solving problems with other children.
At work time, when Glen said he was sad because the snow in the table was starting to melt, Trey put his arm around him and said, "That's okay, I'll play with you again outside where it's colder."	I. Understanding and expressing feelings: (5) Child responds appropriately to the feelings of others.

Continued on the next page.

Continued from the previous page.

CREATIVE REPRESENTATION

Teacher's Anecdotal Notes	*High/Scope COR Item and Level*
At small-group time Ruthi taped a wadded-up piece of paper to the top of a toilet paper roll, then taped a green paper dot and a red paper dot to the roll. She said it was "to protect her from the night monsters. Green turns it on. Red turns it off."	J. Making and building: (5) Child uses materials to make or build things with at least three details represented.
Given ink pads and stickers of **Winnie-the-Pooh** characters, Abby took the ink pad, pressed her fingers on it, and made fingerprints on the paper.	K. Drawing and painting: (2) Child explores drawing and painting materials.
At work time, as Victor and Daniel were rolling on the floor, Jordan went to the block area holding a plastic tube in his hand. Shaking the tube, he said, "I have the power."	L. Pretending: (2) Child uses one object to stand for another and uses actions and sounds to pretend.
At planning time, Glen drew a rectangle and then drew a face in the middle of it that included eyes, a nose, and a mouth. He said to his teacher, "That's me playing with the TV in the block area."	K. Drawing and painting: (4) Child draws or paints representations with a few details.

MUSIC AND MOVEMENT

Teacher's Anecdotal Notes	*High/Scope COR Item and Level*
At small-group time Kacey played "catch" with Julia, catching balls that Julia rolled down the hill to her and throwing the balls back up to Julia.	M. Exhibiting body coordination: (3) Child alternates feet while walking up the stairs without holding on to the banister; tosses and catches a ball or a bean bag.
After rolling down the hill at small-group time, Victor rolled halfway back up the hill.	M. Exhibiting body coordination: (5) Child engages in complex movements.
At work time, Saraya inserted the taped stories into the recorder. She changed the tape once when she wanted to listen to a different story.	N. Exhibiting manual coordination: (3) Child fits materials together and takes them apart.
At work time, as Michael beat a drum and Tanuka sang, "One and, two and, three," Sue tapped her fingers and hopped to the beat of their music.	O. Imitating movements to a steady beat: (4) Child responds to the beat of songs or instrumental music with more complex movements.
At work time Tanuka told Michael that it was his turn to dance but that he first had to put away the drum and get his party clothes and shoes on. In response, Michael put away the drum, stuck a hat on his head, and put on a pair of high-heeled shoes.	P. Following music and movement directions: (4) Child follows spoken instructions for more complex sequences of movements.

LANGUAGE AND LITERACY

TEACHER'S ANECDOTAL NOTES	HIGH/SCOPE COR ITEM AND LEVEL
At large-group time, when Trey suggested that everyone pretend to "melt like a snowman," Kayla said, "Okay, then next let's pretend we're snowflakes, so we can build him back up."	Q. Understanding speech: (4) Child participates in ordinary classroom conversation.
At small-group time Ruthi made a "monster protector." When asked how it worked, she said, "You push this green button, the light comes on, and the monster gets afraid and runs away."	R. Speaking: (4) Child uses sentences that include two or more ideas with descriptive details.
At planning time Taryn was the first child to mention the letters on the "HUNNY POT." She said, "What do those letters spell?"	S. Showing interest in reading activities: (3) Child asks people to read stories or signs or notes.
At work time Micah wrote the letters **P-o-o-h**, copying them from the shirt on the Pooh bear, and taped the word to her own teddy bear from home.	V. Beginning writing: (3) Child copies or writes identifiable letters, perhaps including own name.

LOGIC AND MATHEMATICS

TEACHER'S ANECDOTAL NOTES	HIGH/SCOPE COR ITEM AND LEVEL
At small-group time, Shelby pasted all the stickers that were in his basket on the right side of his paper and used the ink stamps on the left side only.	W. Sorting: (3) In sorting, child groups objects together that are the same in some way but different in other ways.
At greeting time when comparing the two different-sized versions of the book **Who's in the Shed?** Patrick said, "This bear is more scary 'cause he's bigger."	Z. Using comparison words: (4) Child uses comparison words correctly.
At recall time, after recalling near the owl in the tree, Krista pointed out that only five children had turns at recall when there are seven children in the group.	AA. Comparing numbers of objects: (5) Child correctly compares the sizes of groups of more than five objects.
When Victor grazed his shoulder during their Power Ranger play, Daniel shouted, "Don't stand so close to me next time."	CC. Describing spatial relations: (3) Child uses words that describe the relative positions of things.
"I rolled down the fastest," said Trey to Glen at small-group time, "'cause first I climbed the hill and put my hands under my jacket, and then I rolled really fast." (Trey and Glen were having a rolling race down the hill.)	DD. Describing sequence and time: (3) Child describes or represents a series of events in the correct sequence.

Adult Training Activities

This training activity is designed to encourage teaching teams to explore the reactions they have when children imitate the actions of characters from television programs and movies they view outside of school hours.

1. Have members of each teaching team work together in pairs or small groups. Pass out a discussion sheet containing the following three scenarios. Instruct the teaching teams to discuss the strategies they would use in each situation, noting their responses in the space provided under each situation. Teams should discuss the following factors with reference to each situation:

   - Specific materials you might add to the classroom

   - Ways you can take part in children's play without altering the child's original idea

   - Reasons the play has value from the perspective of the High/Scope key experiences or the High/Scope Child Observation Record (COR)

Scenario One:

> *Every day at planning time for the past two weeks, Adam and Christopher make the same plan—to play Batman and Robin. Even though you ask them what they will do as Batman and Robin, they provide no further details. Each day when they start playing, they bring you scarves and ask you to tie them around their necks. Then they spend then next five to ten minutes running back and forth from one end of the room to the other. You notice that after that, they usually start working in other areas, continuing to wear the scarves (which they call "capes") and calling themselves Batman or Robin.*

Scenario Two:

Every morning Daniel and Victor come to school with action figures they bring from home. You ask that they play with them only at greeting time, putting them in their cubbies before planning begins. Since they share the figures readily with others and you notice that this creates a lot of conversation among the children, you are comfortable with this policy. Children seem to follow your rule for a while, but recently you've noticed that they now want to include the figures in their work time plans. Even though your rule about keeping them in the cubbies is still in force, at work time you often find children huddled next to the cubbies playing with action figures.

Scenario Three:

*At least once during every cleanup time this week, Donald has run roaring into Japera, knocking her down to the floor. Each time this has happened she has cried out for adult help. Donald always responds by explaining that he's just the "bad guy" from **Beauty and the Beast** and that he has to knock her over.*

Index

W

About the Author

Michelle Graves, a writer and educational consultant at High/Scope Educational Research Foundation has designed and conducted training workshops and long-term training projects for teachers, teacher-trainers, and educational administrators in a wide range of educational settings, including Head Start and other preschool programs, child care programs, and special education settings. She is also the author of *Daily Planning Around the Key Experiences,* the previous book in *The Teacher's Idea Book* series, and the script author/coproducer of the video-tape *Supporting Children's Active Learning: Teaching Strategies for Diverse Settings* and the *Small-Group Times* videotape series, both from High/Scope Press. Formerly, Graves directed a child care center for employees of the

Veterans Administration Medical Center, Ann Arbor, Michigan, a program serving families with children aged six weeks to five years. She has also had extensive early childhood teaching experience. In addition to the High/Scope Demonstration Preschool, Graves has taught in public and private child care and special education programs.